WONDERDADS

THE BEST DAD/CHILD
ACTIVITIES IN MILWAUKEE

CONTACT WONDERDADS

WonderDads books may be purchased for educational and promotional use. For information, please email us at store@wonderdads.com.

If you are interested in partnership opportunities with WonderDads, please email us at partner@wonderdads.com.

If you are interested in selling WonderDads books and other products in your region, please email us at hiring@wonderdads.com.

For corrections, recommendations on what to include in future versions of the book, updates or any other information, please email us at info@wonderdads.com.

©2011 WonderDads, Inc.

Book Authored by Josh Olson & the WonderDads Staff.

Cover & Book Design by Crystal Langle. Proofread by Jarrod Graham & the WonderDads Staff.

All rights reserved. Printed in the United States of America.

ISBN: 978-1-935153-65-8
First Printing, 2011
10 9 8 7 6 5 4 3 2 1

WONDERDADS MILWAUKEE
Table of Contents

pg. **9**
The Best of Milwaukee

pg. **13**
The Best Dad/Child Restaurants

pg. **39**
The Best Dad/Child Activities

pg. **67**
The Best Dad/Child Stores

pg. **85**
The Best Dad/Child
Outdoor Parks & Recreation

pg. **105**
The Best Dad/Child
Unique Adventures

pg. **119**
The Best Dad/Child
Sporting Events

WELCOME TO WONDERDADS MILWAUKEE

Like so many other Dads, I love being with my kids, but struggle to find the right work/home balance. We are a part of a generation where Dads play much more of an active role with their kids, yet the professional and financial strains are greater than ever. We hope that the ideas in this book make it a little easier to be inspired to do something that makes you a hero in the eyes of your children.

This part of our children's lives goes by too fast, but the memories from a WonderDads inspired trip, event, meal, or activity last a long time (and will probably be laughed about when they grow up). So plan a Daddy day once a week, make breakfast together every Saturday morning, watch your football team every Sunday, or whatever works for you, and be amazed how long they will remember the memories and how good you will feel about yourself in the process.

Our warmest welcome to WonderDads.

Sincerely,

Jonathan Aspatore, **Founder & Dad**
Charlie (4) and Luke (3)

TOP 10 OVERALL BEST DAD/CHILD THINGS TO DO

Betty Brinn Children's Museum . . . . .pg. 40

Discovery World . . . . .pg. 41

Brewers Game at Miller Park . . . . .pg. 122

Adventure Rock Climbing Wall . . . . .pg. 53

Lake Park . . . . .pg. 87

Henry Maier Festival Park . . . . .pg. 42

Kopp's Frozen Custard . . . . pg. 23, 25, 30

Milwaukee County Zoo . . . . .pg. 96

Bradford Beach . . . . .pg. 86

Bristol Renaissance Faire . . . . .pg. 58

TOP 5 DAD/CHILD RESTAURANTS

Kopp's Frozen Custard . . . . pg. 23, 25, 30
Sil's Drive Thru Café. . . . . .pg. 22
Alterra at the Lake. . . . . .pg. 14
Frank's Diner . . . . .pg. 34
Organ Piper Pizza . . . . .pg. 30

TOP 5 DAD/CHILD ACTIVITIES

Betty Brinn Children's Museum . . . . .pg. 40
Discovery World. . . . . .pg. 41
Adventure Rock Climbing Wall. . . . . .pg. 53
Take in a festival at Henry Maier Festival Park . . . . .pg. 42
South Shore Farmer's Market . . . . .pg. 53

TOP 5 DAD/CHILD OUTDOOR PARKS AND RECREATION

Outdoor ice skating at Red Arrow Park . . . . .pg. 88
Boerner Botanical Gardens . . . . .pg. 91
Milwaukee County Zoo . . . . .pg. 96
Birds of Prey at Schlitz Audubon Nature Center. . . . . .pg. 86
Wehr Nature Center . . . . .pg. 94

TOP 5 DAD/CHILD THINGS TO DO ON A RAINY DAY

Betty Brinn Children's Museum . . . . .pg. 40
Discovery World. . . . . .pg. 41
Times and Rosebud Cinemas . . . . .pg. 56
Fun World. . . . . .pg. 95
Paradise Landing Indoor Water Park .pg. 89

TOP 5 DAD/CHILD THINGS TO DO ON A HOT DAY

Bradford Beach . . . . .pg. 86

Cool Waters Family Aquatic Park. . . . . .pg. 94

Bike along the Oak Leaf Trail. . . . . .pg. 89

The Big Backyard. . . . . .pg. 102

Monkey Joe's Indoor Inflatable Playground . . . . .pg. 63

TOP 5 DAD/CHILD FULL-DAY ACTIVITIES

Wisconsin State Fair. . . . . .pg. 56

Lambeau Field Tour and Bay Beach
Amusement Park in Green Bay. . . . . .pg. 113

Little Ammericka . . . . .pg. 116

Circus World . . . . .pg. 116

Old World Wisconsin. . . . . .pg. 64

TOP 5 DAD/CHILD SPLURGES

Brewers game at Miller Park. . . . . .pg. 122

Bristol Renaissance Faire. . . . . .pg. 58

Six Flags Great America and Hurricane Harbor . . . . .pg. 102

Snowtubing at Sunburst Ski Area . . . . .pg. 99

Wisconsin Badgers Football Game at Camp Randall. . . . .pg. 122

TOP 5 DAD/CHILD MOST MEMORABLE

Geocaching/Letterboxing in Lake Park. . . . . .pg. 87

Kite flying with Gift of Wings. . . . . .pg. 68

Downtown Carriage Ride. . . . . .pg. 106

Dog Sledding in Whitnall Park. . . . . .pg. 111

Keno or Hi-Way 18 Drive-In Theaters. . . . . pg. 60, 63

THE BEST OF MILWAUKEE

THE BEST DAD/CHILD
RESTAURANTS

ALTERRA AT THE LAKE

Downtown/Third Ward/Central

1701 N Lincoln Memorial Dr.
Milwaukee, WI 53202
414-223-4551 | www.alterra.com

Not technically a "restaurant," but then again, WonderDads aren't ones to be held back by definitions. Anyways, Alterra offers up coffee-shop hipster fare like quiche and avocado BLTs, but it also serves up a mean grilled cheese and Sprecher root beer. Grab whatever – it's all good – and sit outside of this converted 19th century cream city brick flushing station and enjoy the constant goings-ons of foot traffic along Lake Park with the kids.

ANGELO'S PIZZA

Downtown/Third Ward/Central

1611 W Wells St.
Milwaukee, WI 53233
414-933-4200 | www.angelospizzamilwaukee.com

Close to the Marquette campus, Angelo's offers quality pizza in a tavern atmosphere. It's been there since 1956. They must know what they're doing.

ANMOL PAKISTANI RESTAURANT

Downtown/Third Ward/Central

711 W Historic Mitchell St.
Milwaukee, WI 53204
414-672-7878

Offering large portions at good prices, don't judge Anmol by its atmosphere but rather for the quality of its food. You can't go wrong with the chicken biryani, but if the kids aren't digging it, fill them up on the excellent naan while you polish it off.

BOMBAY SWEETS

Downtown/Third Ward/Central

3401 S 13th St.
Milwaukee, WI 53215
414-383-3553 | www.bombaysweetsmilwaukee.com

Cheap Indian food in this no-frills restaurant that also has a large selection of Indian sweets and mixed nuts available at the counter. The Gulab Jamun is not for your picky eaters.

BUCA DI BEPPO

Downtown/Third Ward/Central

1233 N Van Buren St.
Milwaukee, WI 53202
414-224-8672 | www.bucadibeppo.com

This chain restaurant offers big family-style servings of Italian food in a "traditional" setting where you'll never have to worry about upsetting the other guests. It's loud, busy, and the sheer amount of pictures and assorted knick-knacks lining the walls and tables in the place will keep your kids entertained for at least fifteen minutes.

THE DOGG HAUS
Downtown/Third Ward/Central

1633 W Wells St.
Milwaukee, WI 53202
414-933-9179
324 E Wisconsin Ave.
Milwaukee, WI 53202
414-226-2664

Kids love hot dogs. Build your own hot dog with a selection of toppings that will satisfy most anyone. Or have an Italian beef if you're not most anyone. There are also two East Side locations on Brady and Downer Streets.

KARL RATZSCH'S RESTAURANT
Downtown/Third Ward/Central

320 E Mason St.
Milwaukee, WI 53202
414-276-2720 | www.karlratzsch.com

This German restaurant offers up the best German food in Milwaukee and is complemented by antlers on the wall and dirndl-wearing hostesses. It's a bit pricey – and they have real linen tablecloths – but it's a great pick for a special occasion. Tired of Kids' Menus with the chicken fingers, grilled cheeses, and burgers? Well, Ratzsch's has all that. But it also has weinerschnitzel.

LAKEFRONT BREWERY PALM GARDEN
Downtown/Third Ward/Central

1872 N Commerce St.
Milwaukee, WI 53212
414-273-8300 | www.cafevecchio.com

The Lakefront Palm Garden offers the best fish fry ambiance in Milwaukee every Friday night. A polka band plays and brewery tours are offered while you eat in a converted warehouse situated along the Milwaukee River.

MADER'S
Downtown/Third Ward/Central

1041 N Old World 3rd St.
Milwaukee, WI 53203
414-271-3377 | www.madersrestaurant.com

Mader's German restaurant is old. It's been around since 1902. There are suits of armor, swords, and axes on display and its brunch is the stuff of legends – pass on the French toast and scrambled eggs and dig straight into the Bavarian sauerbraten and Hungarian goulash. Have a knackwurst if you're still hungry. Make sure you call ahead and make a reservation.

MILWAUKEE PUBLIC MARKET

Downtown/Third Ward/Central

400 N Water St.
Milwaukee, WI 53202
414-336-1111 | www.milwaukeepublicmarket.com

The Public Market has enough food stalls to satisfy most anyone's cravings (My vote goes to Aladdin's Taste of the East.) and there's a dining area up on the 2nd floor if you're planning on eating there. Be sure to check out the $1 books in the upstairs library cart...you pay for them on the honor system. The market has a free hour of parking in the attached lot with validation and outdoor stalls along the sidewalk during the weekends in the summer.

NORTH POINT CUSTARD STAND

Downtown/Third Ward/Central

2400 Lincoln Memorial Dr.
Milwaukee, WI 53211
414-258-7885 | www.northpointcustard.com

North Point Custard is an old-style custard and burger stand located just south of Bradford Beach. Don't be fooled though, as it has a menu created by a James Beard Foundation award-winner (they're like Oscars for chefs) and along with the traditional fare of burgers and fries, you can also find fried perch and portobello mushroom sandwiches. Save room for the custard too. Breakfast is served Saturday and Sunday mornings and there's also a location in Milwaukee's Mitchell Airport main terminal.

REAL CHILI

Downtown/Third Ward/Central

Two locations:
419 E Wells St.
Milwaukee, WI 53202
414-271-4042
1625 W Wells St.
Milwaukee, WI 53233
414-342-6955

This is no frills eating on a stool at the counter. Pick mild, medium, or hot chili over a bed of spaghetti noodles or beans (or both!). Nothing beats it on a cold winter day.

SAFE HOUSE
Downtown/Third Ward/Central

779 N Front St.
Milwaukee, WI 53202
414-271-2007 | www.safe-house.com

A Milwaukee classic, the Safe House is a spy-themed restaurant located down an alley with not much in the way to announce its presence save for the International Exports Ltd. sign. Gain entrance and you're transported to a world of 1960s Cold War spy movie kitsch. There's a magician on the weekends and a Junior Spies menu.

SOBELMAN'S PUB AND GRILL
Downtown/Third Ward/Central

1900 W Saint Paul Ave.
Milwaukee, WI 53233
414-931-1919 | www.milwaukeesbestburgers.com

Sobelman's is proud of its burgers (check out its website address for Pete's sake)—and rightfully so. Located in an old Schlitz tavern in an out of the way location north of Marquette, Sobelman's stays crowded due to its lively atmosphere, friendly staff, and signature burgers.

SOUP'S ON!
Downtown/Third Ward/Central

221 N Water St.
Milwaukee, WI 53202
414-283-9244 | www.soupsonat221.com

A Sprecher root beer, 16 oz. crock of soup, and hunk of sourdough are the cake. The twenty odd varieties of hot sauce are the icing. This hole-in-the-wall overlooking the Milwaukee River offers four freshly made soups every day and is open for breakfast and lunch only. Closed Saturdays and Sundays.

SPEED QUEEN BAR-B-Q
Downtown/Third Ward/Central

1130 W Walnut St.
Milwaukee, WI 53205
414-265-2900 | www.foodspot.com/speedqueen

Milwaukee's best Bar-B-Q is served in a Styrofoam container with plastic utensils from behind a bulletproof glass order window. If you think that you and the kids can handle it, it's worth a stop for the "outside"—crispy pieces of shoulder meat served up in a tangy sweet sauce with white bread and coleslaw. A drive-thru window is also available.

RESTAURANTS

STREET-ZA PIZZA TRUCK

Downtown/Third Ward/Central

Various locations
www.streetza.com

Ever had pizza out of the side of a truck? I hadn't either. Ever had a slice of pizza topped with spaghetti? It was a first for me too. Street-za offers up great pizza and there's always a slice of the unexpected among its more traditional fare. It's definitely worth tracking down – check the website or follow it on Twitter or Facebook for daily locations.

TIGERBITE FOOD TRUCK

Downtown/Third Ward/Central

Various downtown locations
www.tigerbitetruck.com

Try some Asian-Mexican fusion from the side of this mobile food truck. It's seasonal, and its location varies daily, but check out the website or follow it on Twitter or Facebook to track it down. The menu is limited, but it's not necessary as the tacos – pick from beef, chicken, and pork – are super fresh and will knock your socks off. Call ahead and place your order and they'll have it ready for you when you swing by.

TLC SOUP COMPANY

Downtown/Third Ward/Central

324 E Michigan St.
Milwaukee, WI 53202
414-277-7687

The best soup place in Milwaukee. Plus a big hunk of sourdough bread. Yum. The menu changes daily and there are enough choices that there's something for everyone.

WATTS TEA SHOP

Downtown/Third Ward/Central

761 N Jefferson St.
Milwaukee, WI 53202
414-290-5720 | www.georgewatts.com

Whatever you do, don't be a bull in this place. Sitting above George Watts and Son's china and crystal shop, the tea shop is a perfect spot for a WonderDad and his girls. Have a finger sandwich and don't forget to stick out your pinky as you sip away. If you forget, you can call and arrange for an etiquette course for children. Really.

BEANS AND BARLEY
East Side/Riverwest/Brewers Hill

1901 E North Ave.
Milwaukee, WI 53202
414-278-7878 | www.beansandbarley.com

A specialty grocery store, deli, and café, Beans and Barley serves up healthy food—either to eat-in or to go—and also has a few chairs and tables out front. Its smallish parking lot hosts the East Side Green Market on Saturdays during the summer.

CAFÉ HOLLANDER
East Side/Riverwest/Brewers Hill

2608 N Downer Ave.
Milwaukee, WI 53211
414-963-6366 | www.cafehollander.com

The Hollander's fries (they call them "frites") are the best Milwaukee has to offer, and an assortment of dipping sauces from mayonnaise to peanut sauce to remoulade are available. This place has busy parents in mind too, with the game and kid's book shelf and the tasty and cheap kid's menu. There's a second location in Tosa Village.

CHUBBY'S CHEESESTEAKS
East Side/Riverwest/Brewers Hill

2232 N Oakland Ave.
Milwaukee, WI 53202
414-287-9999 | www.chubbyscheesesteaks.com

With a menu that includes "cheese whiz" as a cheese topping selection, you know you're in for a fine dining experience.

COMET CAFÉ
East Side/Riverwest/Brewers Hill

1947 N Farwell Ave.
Milwaukee, WI 53202
414-273-7677 | www.thecometcafe.com

Comet specializes in "from-scratch comfort food." Sounds good to me. Handmade cupcakes and cookies? Sounds even better. Your kids will agree as you sit on stools along the counter in this casual yet hip corner restaurant.

19

THE DOGG HAUS

East Side/Riverwest/Brewers Hill

Two Locations:
1433 E Brady St.
Milwaukee, WI 53202
414-727-1224
3116 N Downer St.
Milwaukee, WI
414-332-2810

Kids love hot dogs. Build your own hot dog here with a selection of toppings that will satisfy anyone. There are also two Wells Street locations serving the Marquette campus and downtown area.

FUEL CAFÉ

East Side/Riverwest/Brewers Hill

818 E Center St.
Milwaukee, WI 53212
414-374-FUEL | www.fuelcafe.com

Bright and hip, Fuel Café is kid-friendly and offers great sandwiches, from a classic PB & J for those picky eaters to a Wasabi Veggie Melt for the more adventurous. Plenty of vegan and vegetarian options as well if that's your bag.

IAN'S PIZZA BY THE SLICE

East Side/Riverwest/Brewers Hill

2035 E North Ave.
Milwaukee, WI 53202
414-727-9200 | www.ianspizza.com

No-nonsense pizza by the slice. Your kids will get the pepperoni. Wonder-Dad will opt for the spinach feta pesto slice. Everyone is happy.

KOPPA'S FULBELI DELI

East Side/Riverwest/Brewers Hill

1940 N Farwell Ave.
Milwaukee, WI 53202
414-273-1273 | www.koppas.com

With sandwiches named the Bread Favre and the Lunklunk, a daily specials menu that uses the Norse names of the week, and an Atari 2600 console set up to play while you wait for your sandwich, this place has everything WonderDads would ever need.

LISA'S FINE FOOD PIZZERIA
East Side/Riverwest/Brewers Hill

2961 N Oakland Ave.
Milwaukee, WI 53211
414-332-6360 | www.lisasfinefoods.net

Lisa's is always in the discussion for the best pizza in Milwaukee, and this unassuming and cozy East Side restaurant has been serving up great thin-crust pizza for over 40 years. It does a busy carry-out and delivery business, but dining in is recommended – bring a handful of quarters for your kids to pick out songs they've never heard of from the jukebox.

MAHARAJA
East Side/Riverwest/Brewers Hill

1550 N Farwell Ave.
Milwaukee, WI 53202
414-276-2250 | www.maharajarestaurants.com

Maharaja serves up great Indian food and is extremely family-friendly. The buffet is definitely worth a visit.

PIZZA SHUTTLE
East Side/Riverwest/Brewers Hill

1827 N Farwell Ave.
Milwaukee, WI 53202
414-289-9993 | www.pizzashuttle.com

Don't let the name fool you—Pizza Shuttle serves up most anything Won-derDads could want to eat. The menu is absolutely ridiculous. It's cheap and they deliver. Have them bring you a pint of ice cream with the order and it's perfect for a WonderDads movie night with the kids. Think they're ready to be introduced to Raiders of the Lost Ark? I think so. Thank you, Pizza Shuttle.

SATELLITE CREPES
East Side/Riverwest/Brewers Hill

Various locations in Downtown area and East Side
www.satellitecrepes.com

This custom-built "green" food cart—it has a solar-powered fridge and a propane stove—makes tasty fresh crepes (both sweet and savory) on the spot. Your kids will love the experience of choosing their own batter and fillings. Check the website or their Facebook page for locations and schedules.

SIL'S DRIVE-THRU CAFÉ

East Side/Riverwest/Brewers Hill

1801 E North Ave.
Miwaukee, WI 53202
414-225-9365

Architecturally speaking, the place looks like it was made by Magneto during a temper tantrum with its twisted metal beams jutting out in all directions. Forget all that and sidle up to the window (there's not indoor seating) and order up some mini-donuts. They make them to order—you see them drop the batter into a sizzling fryer right through the window—and they're delivered piping-hot.

ZAFFIRO'S PIZZA

East Side/Riverwest/Brewers Hill

1724 N Farwell Ave.
Milwaukee, WI 53202
414-289-8776 | www.zaffirospizza.com

Zaffiro's is small – and it used to be even smaller (the dining room to the right of the entrance is a converted former barber shop) – but it's home to arguably the best pizza in Milwaukee. Be prepared to wait for a seat, or order take out if you're in a hurry.

BENJI'S DELI

North Short & North City

4156 N Oakland Ave.
Shorewood, WI 53211
414-332-7777

Home to the best Reuben in Milwaukeeland, Benji's serves up mountains of meat in this no-frills deli located in a somewhat bedraggled Northshore strip mall. Ignore the atmosphere—the food does most all of the talking.

HIGHLAND HOUSE

North Short & North City

12741 N Port Washington Rd.
Mequon, WI 53092
262-243-5844 | www.highlandhouse.ws

There's no haggis to be had at the Highland House, but rather a mix of Caribbean and Mexican cuisine in this colorful and casual restaurant. It's noisy—you'll never have to worry that your kids will be too loud—and the menu is expansive enough that you can find something for everyone. Try the outdoor patio during the summer.

JAKE'S DELICATESSEN

North Short & North City

1634 W North Ave.
Milwaukee, WI 53205
414-562-1272 | www.jakesmilwaukee.com

Jake's website doesn't mess around. It's just the menu. Its corned beef sandwich doesn't mess around either. It's just a heaping pile of meat, hand sliced to order, on rye bread. Kapow! It's unlikely that the your kids will be able to open their mouths wide enough to get a whole bite...but they'll have fun trying.

JO'S CAFÉ

North Short & North City

3519 W Silver Spring Dr.
Milwaukee, WI 53209
414-461-0210

This place is small. Four tables and a counter small. But the food is big. Homemade apple jelly and cinnamon rolls. Their signature hoffel poffel breakfast is a mash–up of scrambled eggs, salami, potatoes, onions, and cheese, served hot right off of the big grill that's front and center behind the counter.

KOPP'S FROZEN CUSTARD

North Short & North City

5373 N Port Washington Rd.
Milwaukee, WI 53217
414-961-2006 | www.kopps.com

A Milwaukee institution, Kopp's is a classic that serves up great burgers, fries, and onion rings with a staff attired in white outfits and hats straight out of the 1950s. Its custard is among the best to be found and they of-fer a regular change of special and seasonal flavors. Not to be missed!

MR. PERKIN'S FAMILY RESTAURANT

North Short & North City

2001 W Atkinson Ave.
Milwaukee, WI 53209
414-447-6660

Don't confuse this place with the national chain—this is a Milwaukee original that serves up the best soul food in town. The cornbread, baked chicken, and mac 'n' cheese are highlights that WonderDads can get behind.

23

SILVER SPRING HOUSE
North Short & North City

6655 N Green Bay Ave.
Glendale, WI 53209
414-352-3920 | www.silverspringhouse.us

Silver Spring House has been around since 1904 and definitely looks the part. The food is standard Wisconsin tavern offerings with an all you can eat Fish Fry on Fridays. Children eat free on Sundays and Mondays, and there's free pizza at halftime during Packers games.

SOLLY'S GRILLE
North Short & North City

4629 N Port Washington Rd.
Milwaukee, WI 53212
414-332-8808 | www.foodspot.com/sollys

Solly's is always in the discussion over the best burgers in Milwaukee, and I suppose how it will rate depends on how much you like your burger slathered in butter. Their hot dogs and brats get the same treatment.

THE CHANCERY
South Side/Fifth Ward/Walker's Point

4624 S 27th St.
Milwaukee, WI 53221
414-282-3350 | www.thechancery.com

The Chancery offers food that both kids and adults can get into from its six Milwaukee – area locations. Tuesdays are Kids Days, where kids 10 and under pay their height (one penny per inch).

CLASSIC SLICE
South Side/Fifth Ward/Walker's Point

2797 S Kinnickinnic Ave.
Milwaukee, WI 53207
414-238-2406 | www.theclassicslice.com

Classic Slice has made its mark in Bay View as a low-key, family-friendly place to grab a big slice of pizza. Play Ms. Pac-Man at the arcade cabinet, and there's even a stack of coloring books and crayons over by the cash register to help pass the time while you're waiting for a slice as big as your head.

FERCH'S MALT SHOPPE
AND GRILLE
South Side/Fifth Ward/Walker's Point

Two locations:
5356 Broad St.
Greendale, WI 53129
414-423-1414
Wyndham Village
7740 S Lovers Ln.
Franklin, WI 53132
414-235-3305 | www.ferchsmaltshoppe.com

While WonderDads typically avoid establishments that add superfluous e's to their names, make an exception for Ferch's. They have spinny stools at the counter and mix your custard toppings right in front of you on a big slab of marble. Their hot dogs are also excellent. Oh, and there's always the 3 lbs. burger challenge if you're up to the task. Win or lose, it'll be something that your kids will talk about for years to come.

LA FUENTE
South Side/Fifth Ward/Walker's Point

625 S 5th St.
Milwaukee, WI 53204
414-271-8595 | www.ilovelafuente.com

This Walker's Point Mexican restaurant has some of the best chips and salsa in Milwaukee – they're served fresh and warm and make a perfect pre-dinner snack with the kids while sitting out on the big patio. It gets crowded on the weekends during the summer.

GEORGIE PORGIE'S BURGER AND
CUSTARD HANGOUT
South Side/Fifth Ward/Walker's Point

9555 S Howell Ave.
Oak Creek, WI 53154
414-571-9889 | www.georgieporgie.com

A tree house-themed family burger joint with a 2nd location in Racine, Georgie Porgie's serves up great burgers and custard. Car shows are held outside in the parking lot on Saturdays.

KOPP'S
FROZEN CUSTARD
South Side/Fifth Ward/Walker's Point

7631 W Layton Ave.
Milwaukee, WI 53220
414-282-4312 | www.kopps.com

A Milwaukee institution, Kopp's is a classic that serves up great burgers, fires, and onion rings with a staff attired in white outfits and hats straight out of the 1950s. Its custard is among the best to be found and they offer a regular change of special and seasonal flavors. Not to be missed!

25

LEON'S FROZEN CUSTARD
DRIVE-IN
South Side/Fifth Ward/Walker's Point

3131 S 27th St.
Milwaukee, WI 53215
414-383-1784 | www.leonsfrozencustard.com

The question of who makes the best custard in Milwaukee will never be answered, but Leon's makes a strong claim. Stop by this drive-in – virtually unchanged in look since the '50s—for a custard and a phosphate soda.

MARTINO'S
ITALIAN BEEF
South Side/Fifth Ward/Walker's Point

1215 W Layton Ave.
Milwaukee, WI 53221
414-281-5580

This much-loved Southside restaurant serves up the best Chicago-style dogs in Milwaukee, and the Italian beef is pretty great as well. Don't forget to grab some home-made Rice Krispie treats as you head out the door. The staff is super friendly too!

NITE OWL DRIVE-IN
South Side/Fifth Ward/Walker's Point

830 E Layton Ave.
Milwaukee, WI 53207
414-483-2524

With wooden booths, checkered linoleum floors, excellent malts and shakes, and a criminally underappreciated "Jumbo Burger," Nite Owl just feels right. Order a "Me and My Gal" sundae, a couple of spoons, and dig in together for a memorable afternoon treat.

PACIFIC PRODUCE
South Side/Fifth Ward/Walker's Point

5455 South 27th St.
Greenfield, WI 53221
414-817-0241

A small food court hidden in the back of this Asian supermarket offers Thai carry-out and awesome spicy grilled pork sandwiches from Banh Mi Nhu Y. Make sure to lead the kids past the whole ducks and pig snouts on display at the meat counter and order a mango bubble drink with your order—they'll love sucking up the tapioca balls through their straws.

THE PHILLY WAY   South Side/Fifth Ward/Walker's Point

Two locations:
405 S 2nd St.
Milwaukee, WI 53204
414-273-2355
5430 S Packard Ave.
Cudahy, WI 53110
414-897-8961 | www.thephillyway.com

Serving up authentic Philly cheesesteaks (and one of the few locations in Milwaukee with football memorabilia supporting a team other than the Packers and Badgers), The Philly Way is working-class awesome. Get there early on Monday—the first three customers get a free cheese steak, fries, and soda!

RED ROBIN RESTAURANT   South Side/Fifth Ward/Walker's Point

7575 Edgerton Ave.
Greenfield, WI 53220
414-421-2257 | www.redrobin.com

Free balloons, fun, bright décor, and a very kid-friendly menu make this chain an easy pick for WonderDads looking for a good burger. As chain restaurants go, Red Robin is at the top.

EL REY 1   South Side/Fifth Ward/Walker's Point

1023 S Cesar E Chavez Dr.
Milwaukee, WI 53204
414-643-1640 | www.elreyfoods.com

Located in the back corner of this grocery store is a taqueria that serves up some of the best and cheapest Mexican food in Milwaukee. Brush up on your Spanish and order the tacos de pollo or the quesadilla suiza. There's also a taco stand usually stationed in front of the store that serves up elote (corn on the cob) along with tacos.

ROYAL INDIA   South Side/Fifth Ward/Walker's Point

3400 S 27th St.
Milwaukee, WI 53215
414-647-9600

This unassuming restaurant next to a liquor store in a southside strip mall is quietly making a name for itself for its great food and family-friendly atmosphere. Parking is atrocious so be prepared to park down a side street and walk.

SERB HALL
South Side/Fifth Ward/Walker's Point

5101 W Oklahoma Ave.
Milwaukee, WI 53219
414-545-6030

Serb Hall's Friday fish fry is required eating at least once for anyone from Milwaukee. It's impossible to describe—essentially a mobbed banquet hall filled with seemingly thousands of people at hundreds of tables. Why it's so popular is a bit of a mystery—while logistically impressive, it's pretty standard fish fry fare. As an experience, however, it's unrivaled.

TRANSFER PIZZERIA & CAFÉ
South Side/Fifth Ward/Walker's Point

101 W Mitchell St.
Milwaukee, WI 53204
414-763-0438 | www.transfermke.com

Relatively new to the Milwaukee pizza scene, Transfer has made a name for itself with its excellent pizzas. They have over 40 to choose from—from the classic Margherita to Bob's Special (with avocado).

BLUE'S EGG
West side & Wauwatosa

317 N 76th St.
Milwaukee, WI 53213
414-299-3180 | www.bluesegg.com

Open only for breakfast and lunch, this newcomer is the sister restaurant to the wonderful Maxie's Southern Comfort. They serve grapes to snack on before you order. Your kids will love it!

BOMBAY SWEETS
West side & Wauwatosa

19555 W Blue Mound Rd.
Milwaukee, WI 53005
262-780-2998 | www.bombaysweetsmilwaukee.com

Cheap Indian food in this no-frills, all vegetarian restaurant that also has a large selection of Indian sweets and mixed nuts available at the counter.

BUBBA'S FROZEN CUSTARD
West side & Wauwatosa

1276 Capitol Dr.
Pewaukee, WI 53017
262-695-8189 | www.bubbasfrozencustard.com

This Pewaukee favorite serves up pretty much exactly what you'd expect from a guy named Bubba. Good burgers, good custard (with a flavor of the day), and a friendly staff. Recommended.

CAFÉ HOLLANDER
West side & Wauwatosa

7677 W State St.
Wauwatosa, WI 53213
414-475-6771 | www.cafehollander.com

The bookshelf filled with toys, puzzles, and books make this fun for kids. The Belgian beer selection makes this fun for WonderDad. The surprisingly hip restaurant in Tosa Village is kid-friendly with a kid's menu that offers JELL–O for dessert! There's a second location on Downer Ave. in the East Side.

THE CHANCERY
West side & Wauwatosa

7615 W State St.
Wauwatosa, WI 53213
414-282-3350 | www.thechancery.com

The Chancery offers food that both kids and adults can get into from its six Milwaukee–area locations. Tuesdays are Kids Days, where kids 10 and under pay their height (one penny per inch!) when they order from the Kids Menu!

DAVE AND BUSTER'S
West side & Wauwatosa

2201 N Mayfair Rd.
Wauwatosa, WI 53226
414-454-0100 | www.daveandbusters.com

This national chain offers video games and food, and while it does go after an older crowd with its bar and happy hour, it is also kid-friendly with a kid's menu and plenty of arcade games to keep them entertained. Check the website for promotions such as ½ price games on Wednesdays and Eat and Play combos.

FUDDRUCKER'S
West side & Wauwatosa

Brookfield Square Mall
16065 W Blue Mound Rd.
Brookfield, WI 53005
262-784-3833 | www.fuddruckers.com

While there are a lot of Sobelman's fans who would disagree, this national chain has trademarked the phrase "World's Best Hamburgers." Go figure. Fuddrucker's is kid-friendly and offers big burgers that any WonderDad can get behind. Even better yet, you can also get ostrich, buffalo, and elk burgers.

GILLES FROZEN CUSTARD
West side & Wauwatosa

7515 W Blue Mound Rd.
Milwaukee, WI 53213
414-453-4875 | www.gillesfrozencustard.com

Milwaukee's oldest custard stand—it's been around since 1938—and always on the list of contenders for the title of best custard in Milwaukee.

29

KOPP'S FROZEN CUSTARD
West side & Wauwatosa

18880 W Blue Mound Rd.
Brookfield, WI 53045
262-789-1393 | www.kopps.com

A Milwaukee institution, Kopp's is a classic that serves up great burgers, fries, and onion rings with a staff attired in white outfits and hats straight out of the 1950s. Its custard is among the best to be found and they offer a regular change of special and seasonal flavors. Not to be missed!

MAXIE'S SOUTHERN COMFORT
West side & Wauwatosa

6732 W Fairview Ave
Milwaukee, WI 53213
414-292-3969 | www.maxies.com

This much-loved restaurant serves up Southern food – Cajun, Creole, Soul, Bar-B-Q – and does it well. There's not a stinker on the menu and the cozy, fun atmosphere is kid-friendly. Maxie's gets busy—call ahead and put your name on the list 30 or so minutes before you arrive. Sundays are family nights with $1 kids' meals!

ORGAN PIPER PIZZA
West side & Wauwatosa

4353 S 108th St.
Greenfield, WI 53228
414-529-1177 | www.organpiperpizza.com

A Milwaukee original, Organ Piper Pizza doesn't have great pizza. What it does have, however, is a monster pipe organ and talented organists who can play most anything. Drop a request in the bowl by his elevated bench. My vote's on the Winnie the Pooh title song followed by the Star Wars theme music.

RED ROBIN
West side & Wauwatosa

95 N Moorland Rd
Brookfield, WI 53005
262-641-2313 | www.redrobin.com

Free balloons, fun, bright décor, and a very kid-friendly menu make this chain an easy pick for WonderDads looking for a good burger.

SAMMY'S TASTE OF CHICAGO

West side & Wauwatosa

10534 W Greenfield Ave.
Milwaukee, WI 53214
414-774-0466 | www.sammystasteofchicago.com

It takes a lot for an establishment with the name "Chicago" in it to do well in Milwaukee, but Sammy's does just that with a steady business based on serving up excellent Chicago-style dogs. There's no need to really check out the menu—the Chicago Dog is what you want—and they cost a mere 99 cents on Sundays. Check the website for printable coupons.

SAZ'S STATE HOUSE

West side & Wauwatosa

5539 W State St.
Milwaukee, WI 53208
414-453-2410 | www.sazs.com

A true Milwaukee sports destination with buses that run to and from the restaurant for Bucks, Brewers, Admirals, and Golden Eagles games, Saz's also has a chartered bus that heads to Green Bay for Packers games. Saz is known for its ribs—a junior portion is available on the kids' menu.

STONEFIRE PIZZA CO.

West side & Wauwatosa

5320 S Moorland Rd.
New Berlin, WI 53151
262-970-8800 | www.stonefirepizzaco.com

In the mold of Chuck E. Cheese and Dave and Busters, StoneFire offers a kid-focused assortment of video games, bumper cars, and mini bowling along with buffet-style pizza and food. The kids will love it while you try to hold on to your sanity amid all of the commotion.

TED'S ICE CREAM AND RESTAURANT

West side & Wauwatosa

6204 W North Ave.
Milwaukee, WI 53213
414-258-5610

Unpretentious and inexpensive, Ted's is a classic diner that time forgot. Eat on a stool at the s-shaped counter and dig into the breakfast special. At $4.25 for two eggs, two pieces of bacon, hash browns, and toast, you can't go wrong.

RESTAURANTS

THE CHANCERY

Ozaukee County & Points North

11046 N Port Washington Rd.
Thiensville, WI 53092
262-241-3450 | www.thechancery.com

This Milwaukee chain is fantastically kid-friendly, and with pay your height kids' day on Tuesday, its fantastic on WonderDads' wallets. Plus, the adult menu options are tasty enough to make you want to come back no matter what it costs to fill the kids full of chicken tenders.

THE CHOCOLATE FACTORY SUBS AND ICE CREAM

Ozaukee County & Points North

W62 N577 Washington Ave.
Cedarburg, WI 53012
262-377-8877 | www.subsandicecream.com

While there are Chocolate Factories in several other locations, this one in downtown Cedarburg is the original and best. Serves up warm croissant sandwiches and subs as well as homemade Wisconsin ice cream.

THE FARMSTEAD

Ozaukee County & Points North

W62 N238 Washington Ave.
Cedarburg, WI 53012
262-375-2655

Located in a converted old farmhouse, The Farmstead serves up good food in big portions—the garlic mashed potatoes are a favorite. Be prepared to wait on weekends as it fills up.

HARRY'S RESTAURANT

Ozaukee County & Points North

2128 N Franklin St.
Port Washington, WI 53074
262-284-2861

A Port Washington classic, this diner serves up tasty no-frills breakfast and short-order fare just a block from Lake Michigan.

PASTA SHOPPE

Ozaukee County & Points North

323 N Franklin St.
Port Washington, WI 53074
262-284-9311 | www.portpastashoppe.com

This comfortable family-friendly restaurant serves up great Italian food at good prices. Try the spedini! Crayons are supplied to the kids for drawing on the paper table coverings.

TELLO'S GRILLE & CAFÉ

Ozaukee County & Points North

200 W Grand Ave.
Port Washington, WI 53074
262-268-1133 | www.telloscafe.com

Ostensibly a Mexican restaurant, Tello's menu is eleven pages long and has everything from pizza to gyros to ribs to burgers to pasta to pancakes to stir–fry...and that's not including the unusually extensive kids' menu. It's in a great old building to boot.

WAYNE'S DRIVE-IN

Ozaukee County & Points North

1331 Covered Bridge Rd.
Cedarburg, WI 53012
262-375-9999

Who doesn't like a good drive-in? And especially ones with roller-skating carhops! This classic diner serves up tasty burgers, fries, and shakes. The Wayne Burger is the way to go. Really.

THE CHANCERY

Racine/Kenosha/Points South

Two locations:
11900 108th St.
Pleasant Prairie, WI 53158
262-857-3540
207 Gas Light Cir.
Racine, WI 53407
262-635-0533 | www.thechancery.com

With two locations in this area, the WonderDads south of Milwaukee have no excuse not to check out Kids' Day at The Chancery, when kids 10 and under pay their height (one penny per inch!) when they order from the kid's menu! That's a bargain and a great counting or arithmetic exercise for the kid who's paying.

CHICK-FIL-A

Racine/Kenosha/Points South

Regency Mall
5812 Durand Ave.
Racine, WI 53406
262-554-5009 | www.chickfila.com

Racine has an undeserved reputation, but it is the only city in Wisconsin to have a Chick-fil-A...which is reason enough to pay it a visit. It has the friendliest staff and best kid's meals of any major fast food chain. Alas, it's closed on Sundays.

RESTAURANTS

FRANK'S DINER
Racine/Kenosha/Points South

508 58th St.
Kenosha, WI 53140
262-657-1017 | www.franksdinerkenosha.com

Try a "garbage plate" at this lunch car diner that's been a Kenosha eatery since 1926. It's tight – looks like you're inside a train car—but completely unique and well worth it.

GEORGIE PORGIE'S
Racine/Kenosha/Points South

5502 Washington Ave.
Racine, WI 53406
262-635-5030 | www.georgieporgie.com

A tree house-themed family burger joint with another location in Oak Creek, Georgie Porgie's serves up great burgers and custard. Be sure to eat upstairs to get the proper tree house experience.

KEWPEE HAMBURGERS
Racine/Kenosha/Points South

520 Wisconsin Ave.
Racine, WI 53403
262-634-9601 | www.kewpee.com

Founded in the 1920s and once boasting over 400 franchises, one of only five remaining Kewpees is located in downtown Racine. It's slogan? "Hamburg pickle on top, makes your heart go flippity-flop!" How could you not want to eat a burger there?

MIKE AND ANGELO'S PIZZERIA
Racine/Kenosha/Points South

6214 Washington Ave.
Racine, WI 53405
262-886-1906 | www.mikeandangelos.com

Mike and Angelo's serves up some good thin-crust pizza in Racine and its casual atmosphere and friendly staff is such that you'll never worry about making too much noise or too much of a mess. A double win for WonderDads!

RED ROBIN RESTAURANT
Racine/Kenosha/Points South

6610 Greenbay Rd. Suite #100
Kenosha, WI 53142
262-653-9844 | www.redrobin.com

Free balloons, fun, bright décor, and a very kid-friendly menu make this chain an easy pick for a WonderDad looking for a good burger.

TENUTA'S DELICATESSEN (AND LIQUORS)

Racine/Kenosha/Points South

3203 52nd St.
Kenosha, WI 53144
262-657-9001 | www.tenutasdeli.com

Grab a couple of Italian sausages from the stand out front—preferably with onions, giardinera, and sauerkraut—and grab a seat at one of the outdoor tables with the kids for a great lunch at this incomparable Italian market. Don't forget to duck inside, too—the place is unlike any other—and pick up some of their frozen pasta sauce.

TROLLEY DOGS

Racine/Kenosha/Points South

5501 6th Ave.
Kenosha, WI 53140
262-652-3647 | www.trolleydogs.com

Their signature Trolley Dog is a hot dog topped with a tamale. I'm not sure why no one thought of that before, but it's pure genius. The menu has every variation of hot dog a WonderDads could want. Make sure to check out the model train that does laps around the track on the ceiling.

WELLS BROS. PIZZA

Racine/Kenosha/Points South

2148 Mead St.
Racine, WI 53404
262-632-4408 | www.wellsbrosracine.com

Don't get turned off by the location, as Wells Bros. serves up one of the best thin-crust pizzas in the country. Everything about the place screams old school – it's a true gem – and I cannot recommend a trip enough. Call for reservations as it's crowded on Fridays and Saturdays. Closed Sunday and Monday.

THE CHANCERY

Waukesha County & Points West

2100 E Moreland Blvd.
Waukesha, WI 53186
262-549-1720 | www.thechancery.com

The Chancery's Waukesha County location features the same kid-friendly atmosphere as the other 5 Milwaukee area Chancerys, where tuesdays are kids day and kids pay their height, a penny per inch, for entrees off the kid's menu. Ordering from the lunchbox specials can save Wonder-Dad some pennies on adult offerings, too.

THE MACHINE SHED Waukesha County & Points West

N14 W24145 Tower Pl.
Pewaukee, WI 53188
262-523-1322 | www.machineshed.com

"Dedicated to the American Farmer," the Machine Shed offers up big portions of hearty "farm-style" food. It's also responsible for unleashing chocolate-covered bacon and Krispy Kreme cheeseburgers on the world. The Kids Culinary Adventure program, offered the first and third Wednesday of every month, teaches kids how to mix and measure ingredients, use kitchen gadgets, follow recipes, and learn etiquette.

POP'S FROZEN CUSTARD   Waukesha County & Points West

N87 W16459 Appleton Ave.
Menomonee Falls, WI 53051
262-251-3320 | www.popscustard.com

This old-fashioned soda fountain in the downtown area serves up great custard and butter burgers and always has a steady flow of customers. Limited indoor seating but a large patio area in the summer.

THE BEST DAD/CHILD
ACTIVITIES

BE BONS VIVANTS AT BASTILLE DAYS
KID'S DAY
Downtown/Third Ward/Central

Cathedral Square
Kilbourn Ave. & N Jefferson St.
Milwaukee, WI 53202
414-271-1416 | www.bastilledaysfestival.com

Held over a weekend each July, North America's largest outdoor French-themed festival includes a Kid's Day that includes ballet and cooking lessons, waiter obstacle courses, a dog parade, face painting, soccer, and other activities aimed at turning your kids into ardent Francophiles. Berets and striped shirts are optional but highly encouraged.

BETTY BRINN
CHILDREN'S MUSEUM
Downtown/Third Ward/Central

929 E Wisconsin Ave.
Milwaukee, WI 53202
414-390-KIDS (5437) | www.bbcmkids.org

Weekly workshops, special events, and regular new exhibits are all on display at this wonderful children's museum in downtown Milwaukee. Permanent displays include a construction site, a grocery store, and an art room among others. Admission is free on Thursday nights.

BOCCE AT THE ITALIAN
COMMUNITY CENTER
Downtown/Third Ward/Central

631 E Chicago St.
Milwaukee WI 53202
414-223-2180 | www.italianconference.com

Never played bocce? There are four indoor courts available at the Italian Community Center. Call to make a reservation and enjoy a fine date with your kids.

CLASSIC CHILDREN'S THEATER
AT CENTENNIAL HALL
Downtown/Third Ward/Central

733 N 8th st.
Milwaukee, WI 53233
414-272-7701 | www.wix.com

Performed at the restored Centennial Hall in the Milwaukee Public Library's Central Library, these productions are targeted for ages 3-7 and last around an hour each. This is "community" theater at its finest—they only accept reservations by phone or via email and most shows sell out in advance so make sure to reserve early.

DISCOVERY WORLD
Downtown/Third Ward/Central

500 N Harbor Dr.
Milwaukee, WI 53202
414-765-9966 | www.discoveryworld.com

With a focus on developing a better understanding of technology and the environment, Discovery World is great fun for kids and offers a wide variety of exhibits, displays, and activities. From learning about Les Paul's guitars to lying on a bed of nails to walking through a tunnel surrounded by water in the aquarium, there's something for everybody here. A family program is also offered which includes a variety of hands-on activities like candle-making and crystal-growing.

EAST TOWN MARKET
Downtown/Third Ward/Central

Cathedral Square Park
Kilbourn Ave. & N Jefferson St.
Milwaukee, WI 53202
414-271-1416 | www.easttown.com

Over 100 vendors selling everything from locally grown fruits and veggies, flowers, jams and jellies, cheese, meats, nuts, jewelry, clothes, art, soaps, bread, coffee, and plants. A live band plays and special events like Battle of the Chefs are held most weekends. Saturdays June through October. The market heads indoors to the Discovery World from December through May every second Saturday.

EISNER MUSEUM OF ADVERTISING AND DESIGN
Downtown/Third Ward/Central

208 N Water St.
Milwaukee, WI 53202
414-847-3290 | www.eisnermuseum.org

Interactive, very visual, and designed for the short-attention spanned, the Eisner offers a wide variety of exhibits which has something of interest for everybody. Past exhibits have run the gamut from the art of album covers to the Guinness Beer illustrator to classic movie posters. There's really no excuse not to visit, as it's free for kids 12 and under.

HENRY MAIER FESTIVAL PARK

Downtown/Third Ward/Central

200 N Harbor Dr.
Milwaukee, WI 53202
414-273-3378
www.festaitaliana.com
www.irishfest.com
www.germanfest.com
www.polishfest.com
indiansummer.org
www.arabworldfest.com

Seasonal. Located in downtown Milwaukee along the lake, the festival grounds host not only Summerfest but several additional ethnic festivals to include Polish Fest, Mexican Fiesta, German Fest, Indian Summer, Asian Moon Festival, Arab World Fest, African World Festival, Irish Fest, and Festa Italiana. Irish Fest is the biggest celebration of Irish culture and music in the world, while Festa Italiana and German Fest can only brag of being the largest festivals of their respective cultures in the U.S. Regardless, they're big, fun events with tons of activities, good food, and music.

FIRST STAGE CHILDREN'S THEATER

Downtown/Third Ward/Central

Todd Wehr Theater at the Marcus Center for Performing Arts
929 N Water St.
Milwaukee, WI 53212
414-267-2929 | www.firststage.org

First Stage offers a wide range of plays and performances specifically geared towards children. For season–ticket holders, free Family Workshops are offered before each new performance in the season that offers group explorations of a play's themes that includes acting out scenes from the play and role-playing. Be sure to check the website for recommended ages for the performances. Some performances are also held at the Milwaukee Youth Arts Center (MYAC) in Downtown.

WALK WITH GIANTS IN THE GROHMANN MUSEUM

Downtown/Third Ward/Central

Milwaukee School of Engineering
1000 N Broadway Ave.
Milwaukee, WI 53202
414-277-2300 | www.msoe.edu/museum

The highlight for the kids in this recently opened art museum will certainly be the rooftop sculpture garden with its great view of downtown and the dozen 9-foot tall sculptures (mostly of the rugged and bronzed proletariat wielding big hammers). Children under 12 are free!

GET YOUR MOTOR RUNNIN' AT THE HARLEY-DAVIDSON FACTORY TOUR
Downtown/Third Ward/Central

400 W Canal St.
Milwaukee, WI 53201
1-877-HDMUSEUM | www.harley-davidson.com

The museum is surprisingly family-friendly with an available "Road Pack" that includes activities especially designed for kids. Family Days are held every Sunday where you can get a temporary tattoo. And Glory, a live bald eagle, may be in attendance too! The Motor Restaurant and Café Racer are on-site to tackle power hunger you'll certainly build up after a few hours of looking at rocker arms and crank shafts.

WALKING TOUR WITH HISTORIC MILWAUKEE INCORPORATED
Downtown/Third Ward/Central

Various city locations
414-277-7795 | www.historicmilwaukee.org

Historic Milwaukee, Inc. works to preserve Milwaukee's historical and architectural heritage and offers a series of regular and special walking, biking, and boat tours highlighting a facet of Milwaukee's past. Take a twilight tour and then take the kids to dinner afterwards for being so well-behaved! Kids under 6 are free.

STEP DANCING AT IRISH CULTURAL AND HERITAGE CENTER
Downtown/Third Ward/Central

2133 W Wisconsin Ave.
Milwaukee, WI 53233
414-345-8800 | www.ichc.net

Located in the Grand Ave. Congregational Church, family-friendly Irish dancing is offered the first Friday and third Saturday of every month. Friendly instructors are there to help out if you're not a Lord of the Dance, and it's all done to live music to boot!

JAZZ IN THE PARK
Downtown/Third Ward/Central

Cathedral Square Park
Kilbourn Ave. & N Jefferson St.
Milwaukee, WI 53202
414-271-1416 | www.easttown.com

Grab a blanket, a cooler of food and drinks, and enjoy this free summer outdoor music series in Cathedral Square. Arrive early if you want a decent spot as it fills up. June through September starting at 6pm.

KINDERKONZERTS WITH THE MILWAUKEE SYMPHONY ORCHESTRA Downtown/Third Ward/Central

929 N Water St.
Milwaukee, WI 53202
414-273-7121
www.marcuscenter.org
www.mso.org

The Milwaukee Symphony Orchestra offers a semi-regular Kinderkonzert series on Sunday afternoons with performances specifically geared towards 3 to 12-year-olds. The shows combine storytelling with the music performance and include pre-concert activities such as a book fair, instrument petting zoo, and arts and crafts.

PAJAMA JAMBOREE AT THE MARCUS CENTER FOR THE PERFORMING ARTS Downtown/Third Ward/Central

929 N Water St.
Milwaukee, WI 53202
414-273-7121
www.marcuscenter.org
www.festivalcitysymphony.com

Theater, Ballet, Opera, Symphony, Broadway, Off-Broadway—it can all be found at the performing arts center—and most of it would make the kids squirm in their seats. There are, however, a lot of kid-specific events as well, including the Festival City Symphony's nighttime Pajama Jamborees, Symphony Sundays, and free children's programming at the KidZ Days at the Center series.

MILWAUKEE ART MUSEUM Downtown/Third Ward/Central

700 N Art Museum Dr.
Milwaukee, WI 53202
414-224-3200 | www.mam.org

The Calatrava, a signature landmark on the Milwaukee waterfront, is designed to look like a sailing ship complete with sunscreen "wings" that open and close twice daily. The museum offers tons of great programs that WonderDads can participate in with his kids. The Art Generation program on weekends offers hands-on art activities for kids and parents, and Art-Packs are additionally available any time with activities designed to keep kids interested—they're free with admission. A family audio guide is available which focuses on pieces that will be of interest to kids, and finally, be sure to check out the Partners in Art program, where WonderDads and their kids can create art side-by-side.

MILWAUKEE BALLET'S
NUTCRACKER SUITE
Downtown/Third Ward/Central

929 N Water St.
Milwaukee, WI 53202
414-227-0500
www.marcuscenter.org
www.milwaukeeballet.org

Two events seem to be immutable in Milwaukee come the holidays: the Milwaukee Ballet's Nutcracker Suite and the Harlem Globetrotters at the Bradley Center on New Year's Eve. Rediscover the magic of the season with the kids at this annual performance. As if your daughters needed any more impetus to want to be ballerinas...

TAKE A MUSIC CLASS TOGETHER
AT THE MILWAUKEE CONSERVATORY
OF MUSIC
Downtown/Third Ward/Central

1584 Prospect Ave.
Milwaukee, WI 53202
414-276-5760 | www.wcmusic.org

Most adults have horror stories from their childhood about being forced to take music lessons. Subject your kids to the same at the Milwaukee Conservatory! Or, perhaps, discover that your kid's a child prodigy. The conservatory offers several early childhood and family programs for kids from 4 months to 5 years old to beat on drums and strum guitars together with their WonderDad. Also located in Brookfield and Fox Point.

'SATURDAYS AT CENTRAL' AT THE
MILWAUKEE COUNTY CENTRAL
PUBLIC LIBRARY
Downtown/Third Ward/Central

814 W Wisconsin Ave.
Milwaukee, WI 53233
414-286-3000 | www.mpl.org

The Saturdays at Central program offers a new activity/event each weekend, with programs ranging from reading to pets from the Humane Society to seeing a magic or puppet show. Make sure to take advantage of the twelve excellent public libraries in Milwaukee County, as all offer a variety of events and activities for kids and parents—some unique to the library and some shared across various branches. The searchable calendar on the county library website lists all activities at all the branches.

MITCHELL PARK HORTICULTURAL OBSERVATORY (THE DOMES)
Downtown/Third Ward/Central

524 S Layton Ave.
Milwaukee, WI 53215
414-649-9830 | county.milwaukee.gov/MitchellParkConserva10116.htm
The three domes – the Arid, Tropical, and Floral Show Domes – may be a bit boring for the kids, but head there at night. A major renovation in 2009 fitted the domes with high-powered LED lights that make for a dramatic show. An annual train show in the Floral Show dome is also worth a visit.

THE PATTY AND JAY BAKER THEATER COMPLEX
Downtown/Third Ward/Central

108 E Wells St.
Milwaukee, WI 53202
414-224-9490 | www.milwaukeerep.com
The annual production of A Christmas Carol, a Christmas tradition in Milwaukee since 1975, is not to be missed, but The Rep also occasionally offers family-friendly fare throughout the year at one of its four theaters. Check the website for the schedule and recommended ages/grades for its performances.

MILWAUKEE YOUTH SYMPHONY ORCHESTRA
Downtown/Third Ward/Central

Milwaukee Youth Arts Center
325 W Walnut St.
Milwaukee, WI 53212
414-267-2950 | www.myso.org
Want to see a 3rd-grader rock out on the viola? Want to inspire your kid to be the next Yo-Yo Ma? Go check out a performance at the MYAC—they offer a variety of ensembles and programs.

TWILIGHT TOUR OF THE PABST MANSION
Downtown/Third Ward/Central

2000 W Wisconsin Ave.
Milwaukee, WI 53233
414-931-0808 | www.pabstmansion.com
Built in 1892, this Flemish Revival mansion was home to the founder of the Pabst Brewery and offers Twilight Tours with docents dressed in period attire. It also gets special treatment come the holidays by celebrating a "Grand Ave. Christmas" from November into January, and additionally hosts Dickens Dinners where they serve traditional English holiday fare. Maybe you can even figure out what the heck "figgy pudding" is.

TAKE IN A SHOW AT THE
PABST THEATER
Downtown/Third Ward/Central

114 E Wells st.
Milwaukee, WI 53202
414-286-3663 | www.pabsttheater.org

The Pabst, the fourth-oldest continually operated theater in the U.S., is a Milwaukee landmark and a must-see venue. It offers a few family-friendly shows among its eclectic mix of touring acts—you can even sort the calendar on the website by "Family."

SUMMERFEST!
Downtown/Third Ward/Central

200 N Harbor Dr.
Milwaukee, WI 53202
414-273-2680 | www.summerfest.com

Summerfest is the world's largest music festival, featuring hundreds of performances spanning the course of eleven days. Don't be there at night as it tends to turn into a drunkfest, but during the day there are plenty of kid-friendly activities like magic shows, a huge play area, and lots of good food.

VILLA TERRACE DECORATIVE
ARTS MUSEUMS
Downtown/Third Ward/Central

2220 N Terrace Ave.
Milwaukee, WI 53202
414-271-3656 | www.cavtmuseums.org

Dragging your kid through an Italian Renaissance-style villa cum decorative arts museum is usually a recipe for disaster, and that would be the case the vast, vast majority of the time at Villa Terrace, but the museum does include occasional events for kids including Children's Art in the Garden and Breakfast with Santa events.

WILDCARD GYMNASTICS
OPEN GYMS
Downtown/Third Ward/Central

St. James Lutheran Church Gymnasium
2028 N 60th St.
Milwaukee, WI 53208
414-801-0546 | www.wildcard-gymnastics.com

It's like a jungle gym on steroids with trampolines, mats, balls, ropes, and all sorts of fun things to wear your kids out. Pre-school open gyms are offered on Monday and Friday mornings as well as Friday evenings. Also offers parent-accompanied pre-school classes for kids.

47

DOWNER THEATER
East Side/Riverwest/Brewers Hill

2589 N Downer Ave.
Milwaukee, WI 53211
414-276-8711
www.landmarktheaters.com/market/Milwaukee/DownerTheater.htm
Built in 1915, the Downer is the oldest operating theater in Milwaukee and shows a lot of smaller and independent films. It's a neighborhood theater with limited street parking so be sure to ask the theater staff to refill your parking meter. Make a day of it and stop by the Boswell Book Company and Café Hollander afterwards—both are a stone's throw away.

EAST SIDE GREEN MARKET
East Side/Riverwest/Brewers Hill

Beans & Barley Parking Lot
1901 E North Ave.
Milwaukee, WI 53202
www.theeastside.org
This farmers' market features produce grown within the city of Milwaukee and features live music most weekends. Saturdays from June through October.

ORIENTAL THEATER
East Side/Riverwest/Brewers Hill

2230 N Farwell Ave.
Milwaukee, WI 53202
414-276-8711 | www.landmarktheaters.com
The East Side's Oriental Theater, built in 1927, is the last great golden age theater in Milwaukee. The old place still holds its magic, and is one of the main hosts of the Milwaukee Film Festival each fall. Seeing a movie at the Oriental is a Milwaukee requirement. Originally part of the theater, the Landmark Lanes Bowling Alley is right next door down the steps.

RIVERWEST GARDENERS' MARKET
East Side/Riverwest/Brewers Hill

Garden Park
821 E Locust St.
Milwaukee, WI 53212
www.riverwestmarket.com
What's the difference between a farmers' market and a gardeners' market? The folks in this Riverwest market may be able to tell you as you and the kids shovel down a nutella crepe from the Satellite Crepe mobile food cart. Live music. Sundays from June through October.

UWM PLANETARIUM East Side/Riverwest/Brewers Hill

Manfred Olson Planetarium
1900 E Kenwood Blvd.
Milwaukee, WI 53211
414-229-4961 | www4.uwm.edu/planetarium
Open to the public, the planetarium offers a regular series of programs to include Friday Night Shows, AstroBreaks on selected Wednesdays, and outdoor stargazing on selected weeknights. They additionally occasionally offer special programs such as linking astronomy to The Odyssey, Greek gods and constellations.

ART TROOPER North Shore & North City

East Town Square
11055 N Port Washington Rd.
Mequon, WI 53092
262-241-4343 | www.arttrooper.com
Paint your own pottery, craft a mosaic, or mold some clay. And you don't have to clean up the mess.

BROWN DEER FARMERS' MARKET North Shore & North City

Lowe's parking lot
6300 W Brown Deer Rd.
Brown Deer, WI 53223
Just because you buy some locally grown-organic broccoli at the farmers' market doesn't mean that the kids will eat it. Not, of course, unless you smother it in cheese. Might as well get that, too—it's just three stalls down. Wednesdays May through October.

FOX BAY CINEMA GRILL North Shore & North City

334 E Silver Spring Dr.
Whitefish Bay, WI 53217
414-906-9994 | www.foxbaycinemagrill.com
Situated in downtown Fox Point, the Fox Bay shows first-run movies and serves you dinner while you watch.

49

ACTIVITIES

MILWAUKEE CONSERVATORY OF MUSIC CLASSES
North Shore & North City

8705A N Port Washington Rd.
Fox Point, WI 53217
414-276-5760 | www.wcmusic.org

Instill a love of music in your kids from an early age with classes in just about any instrument you can imagine available through the Milwaukee Conservatory of Music. They offer adult classes too, so you can be the WonderDad who leads by example. Maybe you'll even form a family band! Alternate locations in Downtown Milwaukee and Brookfield.

SCHROEDER AQUATIC CENTER
North Shore & North City

9250 N Green Bay Rd.
Brown Deer, WI 53209
414-357-2834 | wsacltd.org

Lap swim while your kids take swimming and diving lessons. This is a pretty serious facility for competitive swimmers and may not be for everybody, but a certain WonderDad didn't learn to dive until he was 26 and has always regretted not learning sooner. Don't do that to your kids. (P.S. The facility's namesake, Walter Schroeder, is a ghost. Seriously. You can find him in Room 717 in the Ramada Inn in Fond du Lac, Wisconsin. It was featured in NPR's This American Life. They wouldn't lie.)

SPRECHER BREWERY TOUR
North Shore & North City

701 W Glendale Ave.
Glendale, WI 53209
414-964-2739 | www.sprecherbrewery.com/tours.php

Sprecher Root Beer was named the #1 root beer by the New York Times, and the tour covers both the beer and the soda-making processes (They use the same vats for making both!). After the tour, you can sample the eight different sodas on tap. This WonderDad recommends the Ravin' Red.

WATCH PLANES AT TIMMERMAN FIELD
North Shore & North City

9305 W Appleton Dr.
Milwaukee, WI 53225
414-461-3222 | www.flymilwaukee.com

Milwaukee County's general aviation (i.e, small planes) airport has well over 100 take offs and landings a day and is a great spot to take a break with a drive-thru lunch and watch some planes with the kids. Watch from the play area in Madison Park (9800 W Glendale Ave.) just to the south of the airport.

WEST ALLIS FARMERS' MARKET AND MARKET PLACE
North Shore & North City

6501 W National Ave.
West Allis, WI 53214
www.ci.west-allis.wi.us/health/health_farmers_market.htm

This market has all of the standards, including locally grown chickens and fresh eggs. Tuesdays, Thursdays, and Saturdays May through November. The West Allis Market Place—with vendors selling everything from records to antiques to tools—is held Sundays at the same location.

BAY VIEW BOWL
South Side/Fifth Ward/Walker's Point

2416 S Kinnickinnic Ave.
Milwaukee, WI 53207
414-483-0950

Twelve lanes at your disposable, with rentals and a snack bar. Saturday night glow bowl is a great escape with those tweens who think they're too cool to hang with Dad, but still require constant supervision and for you to drive them everywhere.

BOUNCE REALM
South Side/Fifth Ward/Walker's Point

4595 S 27th St.
Greenfield WI 53221
414-281-8000 | www.bouncerealm.com
The name kinda says it all. Closed on Mondays.

CLASSIC CHILDREN'S THEATER AT SOUTHRIDGE MALL
South Side/Fifth Ward/Walker's Point

5300 S 76th St.
Greendale, WI 53129
414-272-7701 | www.wix.com

Performed in the Kids' Clubhouse in the southwest corner of Southridge Mall, these productions are targeted for ages 3-7 and last around an hour each. The mall has a pretty good play area too. The Children's Theater also has performances at Centennial Hall in the Downtown Central Library.

COMEDYSPORTZ
South Side/Fifth Ward/Walker's Point

420 S First St.
Milwaukee, WI 53202
414-272-8888 | www.comedysportzmilwaukee.com

While a lot of the evening fare isn't appropriate for all, the Saturday afternoon comedy shows are specifically geared towards kids. Also hosts birthday parties and kid's events.

ACTIVITIES

KOZ'S MINI BOWL South Side/Fifth Ward/Walker's Point

2078 S 7th St.
Milwaukee, WI 53204
414-383-0560

Your kids may not be aware that bowling outside of WiiSports exists. Starting them out on a mini-version may be a good stepping stone for the real thing. The bowling balls here are mini as in grapefruit-sized.

MIDWEST TWISTERS GYMNASTICS
OPEN GYM South Side/Fifth Ward/Walker's Point

600 E Rawson Ave.
Oak Creek, WI 53154
414-764-6540
11227 W Forest Home Ave.
Franklin, WI 53132
414-425-4655 | www.midwesttwisters.com

Offers open gym, preschool classes, birthday parties, and special events that include anti-gravity night, parents night out, and holiday events. Also locations in Franklin and Hartland.

MITCHELL GALLERY
OF FLIGHT South Side/Fifth Ward/Walker's Point

5300 S Howell Ave.
Milwaukee, WI 53207
414-747-4503 | www.mitchellgallery.org

Located on the concession level of Mitchell Airport, the gallery celebrates Milwaukee's contributions to aviation. Bong. Lovell. Mitchell. You should really know who these guys are. Grab lunch at the Bartolotta-run Northpoint Burgers and Custard in the same terminal while you're there.

QUALITY CANDY/BUDDY SQUIRREL CANDY
AND NUT TOUR South Side/Fifth Ward/Walker's Point

1801 E Bolivar Ave.
St. Francis, WI 53235
414-483-4500 | www.qcbs.com

You'd be nuts to not check out the roasting and popping rooms, to say nothing of kitchens where they prepare the fillings for their chocolates. Not providing samples at the end of the tour would be cruel and unusual —thankfully they do.

ROLLAERO
SKATE CENTER
South Side/Fifth Ward/Walker's Point

4200 S Pennsylvania Ave.
Cudahy, WI 53110
414-747-1414 | www.rollaero-mke.com

When only the best will do, try the maple wood floors at Rollaero for some rollerskating or blading. Rollaero is cash only and there's no ATM is on the premises.

ST. JOSEPHAT
BASILICA TOUR
South Side/Fifth Ward/Walker's Point

2333 S 6th St.
Milwaukee, WI 53215
414-645-5623 | www.thebasilica.org

Can't interest the kids in taking a tour of an old church and seeing one of the largest copper domes in the world? Tell them that St. Josephat was martyred by being hacked to death by a battle-axe wielding mob, then shot, torn apart by wild dogs, and tossed into a river. That may work better. Tours are available after the 10 am Mass on Sundays.

SOUTH SHORE
FARMERS' MARKET
South Side/Fifth Ward/Walker's Point

South Shore Park
2900 S Shore Dr.
Milwaukee, WI 53207
southshorefarmersmarket.com

Overlooking Lake Michigan in South Shore Park in Bay View, this is the best farmers' market in Milwaukee. Live music and shows. Saturdays from June through October.

ADVENTURE ROCK
CLIMBING WALL
West Side & Wauwatosa

21250 Capitol Dr.
Pewaukee, WI 53072
262-790-6800 | www.adventurerock.com

With over 12,000 square feet of climbing surface and heights up to 35 feet, Adventure Rock's indoor climbing walls are something that WonderDads and their kids can really get into. Suitable for ages 5 and up, the Clip'N Go auto belay system allows Dads and kids to quickly start climbing unassisted. Look for a great discount with the three-month Family Climbing membership.

53

ACTIVITIES

BEYOND THE CLASSROOM SERIES AT THE WILSON CENTER FOR THE ARTS
West Side & Wauwatosa

Mitchell Park
19805 W Capitol Dr.
Brookfield, WI 53045
262-781-9470 | www.wilson-center.com

Featuring performances by national and local theater companies, the Beyond the Classroom series at the Wilson Center offers a variety of plays and music performances throughout the year. Check the website for recommended ages, as well as for the visual art, dance, theater, and music classes for babies on up.

GREEK FEST
West Side & Wauwatosa

Wisconsin State Fair Park
8100 W Greenfield Ave.
Milwaukee, WI 53214
414-461-9400 | www.milwaukeegreekfest.com

Held in June, the Greek Fest is one of the few ethnic events not held in downtown's festival park, but rather at the State Fair Grounds. Embarass the kids by loudly pronouncing "gyro" phonetically.

INCREDI-ROLL SKATE AND LASER TAG FAMILY FUN CENTER
West Side & Wauwatosa

10928 W Oklahoma Ave.
Milwaukee, WI 53227
414-545-8444 | www.incredi-rollsk8.com

All-you-can-eat pizza, soda and skating for $9.99 on Fridays and $15 admission for the whole family on Wednesdays are among the deals at Incredi-Roll. Saturday morning skating for 12 and under only (with parents) is a good option for beginning skaters. A bounce house and large arcade round out the experience.

KIDS IN MOTION
West Side & Wauwatosa

14135 W Greenfield Rd.
New Berlin, WI 53151
262-649-3144 | www.kidsinmotionwi.com

With activities designed to promote physical activity, social interaction, and the imagination, Kids in Motion's children's museum-style layout will keep the kids entertained for hours. A Grocery Room, Puzzle Room, Costume Room, Arts and Crafts Center, Construction Room, Music Room, open play area, and laser tag all provide a ton of play options.

MILLER PARK TOUR
West Side & Wauwatosa

1 Brewers Way
Milwaukee, WI 53214
414-902-4005 | milwaukee.brewers.mlb.com/mil/ballpark/tours/index.jsp
Available April through September, Miller Park tours feature the dugout, luxury suite level, press box, and Bob Uecker's broadcast booth. Make sure you check out the statues of Robin Yount and Hank Aaron in the plaza area outside of the park. "How can guys lay off pitches that close?!"

MUSIC CLASSES AT THE MILWAUKEE CONSERVATORY OF MUSIC
West Side & Wauwatosa

19800 W Capitol Dr.
Brookfield, WI 53005
414-276-5760 | www.wcmusic.org
Remember music lessons when you were a kid? Pay it forward by introducing your kid to an instrument that he or she can practice non-stop at all hours of the day or night for the rest of your life. Or at least that's how it will seem at first. They'll thank you later, and you'll eventually get some sleep. Locations also in Downtown Milwaukee and Fox Point.

NATIONAL SOLDIERS' HOME HISTORIC DISTRICT
West Side & Wauwatosa

5000 W National Ave.
Milwaukee, WI 53295
www.soldiershome.org
Ever look south when at a Brewers' game and wonder about that old Addams Family-style tower sticking up through the trees? It's the Civil War-era National Soldiers' Home Historic District—the birthplace of federal veteran care in the United States—and includes a chapel, theater, and library among its 25 buildings. Most of the buildings are currently closed, though restoration efforts are ongoing and an annual tour is conducted. Oh, and the chapel and theater are allegedly haunted.

PALERMO'S PIZZA TOUR AND CAFÉ
West Side & Wauwatosa

3301 W Canal St.
Milwaukee, WI 53208
Café: 414-455-0347
Tour: 414-455-0383
www.palermospizza.com
Dat's da best! Palermo's frozen pizza is made in Milwaukee. Tours of the factory are also available by calling ahead, then swing by the surprisingly-good café attached to the production plant afterwards for a piece of pizza or bowl of soup.

ACTIVITIES

PETTIT NATIONAL ICE CENTER
West Side & Wauwatosa

500 S 84th St.
Milwaukee, WI 53214
414-266-0100 | www.thepettit.com

Lace up for some open skating at the ice center, a U.S. Olympic training facility. There's also curling if that's your bag. Classes for both adults and kids are also offered.

ROSEBUD CINEMA
West Side & Wauwatosa

6823 W North Ave.
Wauwatosa, WI 53213
414-607-9446 | www.timescinema.com

Showing a mix of the new and old (The Goonies! Back to the Future! E.T.!) , the mainstream and the art house, the Rosebud is an independent neighborhood theater that delivers food to your seat...which is actually a red velvet couch. Nice!

TIMES CINEMA
West Side & Wauwatosa

5906 W Vliet St.
Milwaukee, WI 53208
414-453-3128 | www.timescniema.com

WonderDads take educating their children seriously, which is why taking them to a screening of "The Treasure of the Sierra Madre" at the Times is a must-do. Sister-theater to the Rosebud in Wauwatosa, the Times is a great independent Milwaukee neighborhood theater, which also offers Dad Pop.

WISCONSIN STATE FAIR
West Side & Wauwatosa

Wisconsin State Fair Park
8100 W Greenfield Ave.
Milwaukee, WI 53214
800-884-FAIR (3247) | www.wistatefair.com

Tons of activities and shows for kids, including pig races, milking demonstration, and Kiddie Kingdom amusement rides, can all be found during the eleven days of the Wisconsin State Fair. The website includes an overview of all of the food on a stick that's available. A nice touch.

ABOVE AND BEYOND
CHILDREN'S MUSEUM   Ozaukee County & Points North

902 N 8th St.
Sheboygan, WI 53081
920-458-4263 | www.abkids.org

This 10,000-square-foot children's museum includes 12 hands-on exhibits spanning three floors and includes a tree house, music room, sky crawl, and a miniature circus.

THE ARTERY AT THE KOHLER
ARTS CENTER   Ozaukee County & Points North

John Michael Kohler Arts Center
608 York Ave.
Sheboygan, WI 53081
920-458-6144 | www.jmkac.org

Grab some art supplies—glue, scissors, markers, string, and whatever else is on hand—and make something refrigerator-magnet-worthy with the kids at this hands-on art space in the Arts Center. A kid's menu in the ARTCafe will keep their creative juices flowing.

BARTHEL FRUIT FARM   Ozaukee County & Points North

12246 N Farmdale Rd.
Mequon, WI 53121
414-242-2737 | www.barthelfruitfarm.com

Need some fresh herbs? Barthel's is the place to go. Picking your own strawberries, apples, and pumpkins seems almost boring in comparison to picking out some alpine lady's mantle herbs. Barthel's also has sugar snap peas available for picking.

OZAUKEE ICE CENTER   Ozaukee County & Points North

5505 W Pioneer Rd.
Mequon, WI 53097
262-375-6851 | www.ozaukeeicecenter.com

This indoor non-profit rink offers free public skating and skate rentals for just a few dollars.

SKATELAND FAMILY SKATING AND
PLAYING CENTER   Ozaukee County & Points North

7084 Sycamore Dr.
Cedarburg, WI 53012
262-377-7522 | www.skate-land.com/ozaukee.html

Family owned since 1955, Skateland offers reduced-rate family nights on Sunday evenings, dollar snack bar items on Thursdays, and all–you–can–eat pizza and soda night on Fridays. There's also a 10-and-under adventure playground if the kids get tired of skating around in circles.

57

ACTIVITIES

PICK YOUR FAVORITE CHRISTMAS TREE AT THE ANDERSON ARTS CENTER
Racine/Kenosha/Points South

121 66th St.
Kenosha, WI 53143
262-653-0481 | andersonartscenter.com

There's free admission to see the professionally decorated Christmas trees in the main gallery of this 1929 stone and stucco mansion in November and December. The kids probably won't enjoy the regular exhibition schedule throughout the year, but the Arts Center does offer kid's art classes.

APPLE HOLLER
Racine/Kenosha/Points South

5006 S Sylvania Ave.
Sturtevant, WI 53177
262-884-7100 | www.appleholler.com

The orchards and pumpkin patches at Apple Holler are the stuff of childhood legend. They have pears and peaches as well. Check the website for picking dates – Gingergold Apples have a 5-day window for picking so you'd best be ready!

CUT YOUR OWN CHRISTMAS TREE AT BENTZ RD. FARM
Racine/Kenosha/Points South

6109 85th St.
Pleasant Prairie, WI 53158
262-697-9851 | www.bentzroadfarm.com

Bentz also offers pumpkin picking, hay rides and has a petting zoo with reindeer, a zebra, a llama, miniature donkeys, and pot-bellied pigs.

GET THE KIDS KNIGHTED AT THE BRISTOL RENAISSANCE FAIRE
Racine/Kenosha/Points South

12550 120th Ave.
Kenosha, WI 53142
847-395-7773 | www.renfair.com/bristol

Grab a monster turkey leg and head to Elizabethan England...with a few wayward wizards...and the occasional pirate. The Faire has a wealth of kids activities that include the Kids' Kingdom play area, a miniature ship sailing pond, a knighting ceremony, and Robin Hood shows, as well as all-ages events like the Full Armor Joust, Falconer show, Barely Balanced acrobats, and Fire Whip Show. Open weekends during the summer.

SEE REENACTORS AT THE CIVIL WAR MUSEUM
Racine/Kenosha/Points South

5400 1st Ave.
Kenosha, WI 53140
262-653-4140 | www.kenosha.org/civilwar

Make sure your kids can tell the difference between grape and canister artillery shells as well as have a working knowledge of 19th-century bullet extraction and brain surgery techniques during the museums living history events. Be sure to also check out the free hands-on Sunday Fundays that include Civil War-era activities like churning butter, washing clothes with a washboard, wearing scratchy woolen uniforms, and playing some 19th-century games (Look dad! No batteries!).

DINOSAUR DISCOVERY MUSEUM
Racine/Kenosha/Points South

5608 10th Ave.
Kenosha, WI 53140
262-653-4450 | www.kenosha.org/dinosaurdiscovery

The kids can probably tell you the difference between a carcharodontosaurus and a micropachycephalosaurus. That's so easy, dad! Bone up (...sorry...couldn't resist) on dinosaurs at this Kenosha museum that has regular events for kids including the free family-focused Sunday Fundays and Dino Storytelling.

EAST TROY ELECTRIC RAILROAD
Racine/Kenosha/Points South

2002 Church St.
East Troy, WI 53120
262-642-3263 | www.easttroyrr.org

In service from May through October, the state's last electric train service makes ten-mile roundtrip runs between the East Troy Train Depot and the Elegant Farmer in Mukwonago. You can board from either side. A regular dinner train service is offered throughout the season as well.

GREEN MEADOWS PETTING FARM
Racine/Kenosha/Points South

33603 High Dr.
Waterford, WI 53185
262-534-2891 | www.greenmeadowsfarmwi.com

Milk a cow! Ride in a tractor! Play with baby bunnies and chicks! Ride a pony! This petting farm has all of the animals that you'd expect and includes free pumpkin-picking in the fall.

59

ACTIVITIES

JELLY BELLY TOUR
Racine/Kenosha/Points South

Jelly Belly Center
10100 Jelly Belly Ln.
Pleasant Prairie WI 532158
866-868-7522 | www.jellybelly.com

Ride the Jelly Belly Express Train! It's a warehouse tour – no candy is actually manufactured here – but there is still a lot of fun to be had and the kids will have a blast creating their own special flavor combinations at the sample bar in the candy store. An attached snack bar offers a very kids-friendly menu including PB&J, mac and cheese, pizza, and hot dogs.

KENO DRIVE-IN
Racine/Kenosha/Points South

9102 Sheridan Rd.
Pleasant Prairie, WI 53158
262-694-8855 | www.kenodrivein.net

It's doubtful that the kids will stay awake through the second movie – shows start at dusk – but that's no reason not to try. Bring sleeping bags, lawn chairs, blankets, coolers with drinks and food, and make a great evening of it. Don't forget bug spray and a portable FM radio if you plan on watching it outside the car.

KENOSHA PUBLIC MUSEUM HAS MAMMOTHS!
Racine/Kenosha/Points South

5500 1st Ave.
Kenosha, WI 53140
262-653-4140 | www.kenoshapublicmuseum.org

Did you know that the largest, most complete mammoth in North America was excavated in Kenosha County? It's 15,000 years old and has cut marks from stone tools which indicate that it was butchered and eaten by humans. Cavemen 1, Mammoth 0! A replica of the mammoth is on display at the museum.

RACINE CHILDREN'S THEATRE
Racine/Kenosha/Points South

2519 Northwestern Ave. (Highway 38)
Racine, WI 53404
262-633-4218 | www.racinetheatre.org/childrenstheatre

Packy the Elephant introduces each performance at the Racine Theatre Guild in this volunteer-based children's theater that has been a Racine staple since 1933. Hang out with the costumed characters in the lobby after the show. Performances are Fridays and weekends starting in November and running through March.

RACINE GYMNASTICS CENTER
Racine/Kenosha/Points South

2501 Golf Ave.
Racine, WI 53404
262-634-2344 | www.racinegymnastics.com
Open gym, preschool classes, birthday parties, and special events that include anti-gravity night, parents' night out, and holiday events.

EGYPTIAN MUMMY AT THE RACINE HERITAGE MUSEUM!
Racine/Kenosha/Points South

701 Maine St.
Racine, WI 53403
262-636-3926 | www.racineheritagemuseum.org
"Malty," an Egyptian mummy dating from around 300 AD, resides in this former Carnegie library cum museum. There are also permanent exhibits on the Racine Belles, the champion women's professional baseball team from the 1940s, and products from Racine that include Johnson's floor polish, Little Golden Books, the World War II-era M5A1 Stuart Light Tank, and yes, Horlick's Malted Milk. Admission is free.

RACINE PUBLIC LIBRARY STORYTIME
Racine/Kenosha/Points South

75 7th St.
Racine, WI 53403
262-636-9245 | www.racinelib.lib.wi.us
Offering free storytime sessions for kids ranging from birth through ten years old, the RPL also offers Educational Open Play sessions and Saturday Family Stories.

FEED A GIRAFFE AT THE RACINE ZOO
Racine/Kenosha/Points South

2131 N Main St.
Racine, WI 53402
262-636-9189 | www.racinezoo.org
Can you distinguish between a Damara zebra and a Grant's zebra? Impress your kids by pointing out the differences at the small but well-maintained Racine zoo. Giraffe feedings are available for a small fee on a first-come, first-served basis during the summer and there's a playground that's perfect for taking a break and letting the kids run wild for a bit. Admission is cheap ($4 adults and $2 children) and even better yet with Racine County residents receiving $1 admission on Mondays.

ACTIVITIES

TAKE IN A PLAY AT THE RHODE CENTER FOR THE ARTS
Racine/Kenosha/Points South

514 56th St.
Kenosha, WI 53141
262-657-7529 | rhodeopera.org

Recommended for ages 4 and up, the Lakeside Players offer "something for everyone" and the weekend Children's Series presents an eclectic and original schedule of performances on Saturdays and Sunday afternoons. The website includes a "Ghost Stories" section detailing several spooky events that have occurred at the allegedly haunted venue.

READ A BOOK TO A DOG AT THE SOUTHWEST PUBLIC LIBRARY
Racine/Kenosha/Points South

7979 38th Ave.
Kenosha, WI 53141
262-564-6100 | www.mykpl.info

Storytime at a public library is a great free way to get out of the house – especially in the winter – and have some easy fun. The Kenosha Library offers storytimes for both toddlers and pre-schoolers as well as a regular schedule of family events that include Wii for the Family, bilingual storytime, Reading Education Assistance Dogs, and storytime yoga and exercise.

THOMPSON STRAWBERRY FARM
Racine/Kenosha/Points South

14000 75th St.
Bristol, WI 53104
262-857-2353 | www.thompsonstrawberryfarm.com

WonderDads avoid pre-picked and like to get down and dirty. Pick your own strawberries in June, raspberries in August, and pumpkins in October. Messy good fun.

AMERICAN DOJO FAMILY MARTIAL ARTS CLASSES
Waukesha County & Point West

Two locations:
2120 E Moreland Blvd. #5
Waukesha, WI 53186
725 Industrial Ct. Unit C
Hartland, WI 53029
262-542-2888 | www.americandojo.com

American Dojo offers family classes! Take a class with the kids and bond while breaking some boards with a well-executed spin kick.

THE CHILDREN'S PLAY GALLERY
Waukesha County & Point West

440 Wells St., #105
Delafield, WI 53018
262-303-4603 | www.thechildrensplaygallery.com

This much-loved children's museum offers the standards—a grocery store, arts and crafts playroom, construction area, and theater stage—as well the unique: a multi-decked ship! The Play Gallery also offers a robust activity calendar—check the website for details.

ELEGANT FARMER
Waukesha County & Point West

1545 Main St.
Mukwonago, WI 53149
262-363-6771 | www.elegantfarmer.com

Famous for its "Apple Pie Baked in a Bag," Elegant Farmer makes some great pies, applesauce, and CiderBaked Ham. Sure, it's touristy, but it's still worth a stop for the food—and why not pick some apples and go for a hayride with the kids while you're at it?

HI-WAY 18 DRIVE-IN THEATER
Waukesha County & Point West

W6423 Highway 18
Jefferson, WI 53549
920-674-6700 | www.highway18.com

Drive-ins are awesome. Bring pillows and sleeping bags – your kids might not make it through the double feature. This one has a playground in it to boot.

MONKEY JOE'S INDOOR INFLATABLE PLAYGROUND
Waukesha County & Point West

2040 W Blue Mound Rd.
Waukesha, WI 53186
262-549-3866 | www.monkeyjoes.com

Part of a national chain, Monkey Joe's is a great escape during the winter months. There's even an adults area with comfy chairs and TVs to watch.

OLD FALLS VILLAGE
Waukesha County & Point West

N96 W15791 County Line Rd.
Menomonee Falls, WI 53051
262-250-3901 | www.oldfallsvillage.com

See how people lived in the 19th century in this living history museum complete with a log cabin home, school house, barn, railroad depot, and dairy farm. The village plays host to Civil War re-enactors as well as the annual Old Falls Village Days in June.

63

MIDWEST TWISTERS GYMNASTICS
OPEN GYM
Waukesha County & Point West

602 Industrial Ct.
Hartland, WI 53029
262-369-2900 | www.midwesttwisters.com

Offers open gym, preschool classes, birthday parties, and special events that include anti-gravity night, parents night out, and holiday events. Also locations in Franklin and Hartland.

OCONOMOWOC
ARTS CENTER
Waukesha County & Point West

641 E Forest St.
Oconomowoc, WI 53066
262-560-3172 | www.oasd.k12.wi.us

A family series provides regular music and theater performances intended for kids, from opera to ballet to marionettes! Check the website for details.

OLD WORLD
WISCONSIN
Waukesha County & Point West

S103 W37890 Hwy. 67
Eagle, WI 53119
262-594-6301 | www.oldworldwisconsin.wisconsinhistory.org

Take an adult/child workshop and make cornbread and apple crisps in a Dutch oven in this living history museum that features farmhouses, barns, and shops of 19th-century Wisconsin. Open May through October with a lot of special events throughout the season.

THE BEST DAD/CHILD
STORES

STORES

DALY'S PEN SHOP
Downtown/Third Ward/Central

Grand Ave. Mall, 2nd Floor
161 W Wisconsin Ave.
Milwaukee, WI 53203
414-276-8900 | www.dalyspenshop.com

While you probably aren't in the market for the $2,500 horsehair-woven Faber-Castell Pen of the Year, Daly's is a unique store that does offer a selection of pens geared for kids. The kids will certainly stop asking for a Nintendo DS or cell phone once they try out the Lamy ABC children's beginner fountain pen, right?

DOWNTOWN BOOKS
Downtown/Third Ward/Central

327 E Wisconsin Ave.
Milwaukee, WI 53202
414-276-5330 | www.downtownbooksonline.com

A huge selection of used comics, two cats, and three floors of well-organized books make Downtown Books one of the best independent bookstores in Milwaukee. The only drawback? You need a map to navigate its aisles.

GIFT OF WINGS
Downtown/Third Ward/Central

Veterans Park
1010 N Lincoln Memorial Dr.
Milwaukee, WI 53202
414-425-8002 | www.giftofwings.com

These guys take kite-flying seriously. While the Quad-Trac 3-meter Pro Foil is as intimidating as it sounds, there's a huge variety of single-line kites perfect for flying around Veterans Park. A skull and crossbones kite for your son? Check. A sunny dolphin kite for your daughter? Sure thing. WonderDad does it again! The store hosts a New Years day kite flying event (with free hot chocolate!) for the truly intrepid.

MCKINLEY MARINA'S BIKE AND SKATE RENTAL
Downtown/Third Ward/Central

Veterans Park, Next to McKinley Arena South
and Milwaukee Community Sailing Center
Milwaukee, WI 53202
414-273-1343 | www.milwbikeskaterental.com

Rent bikes, surreys, recumbents, in-line skates, and even Segways by the half-hour and cruise along the Oak Leaf Trail through Veterans and Lake Parks on the lakefront. Open Memorial through Labor Day.

RENAISSANCE BOOK SHOP

Downtown/Third Ward/Central

834 N Plankinton Ave.
Milwaukee, WI 53203
414-271-6850

Website? Who needs one? Certainly not the Renaissance. This monstrous bookstore comprises three floors and a basement. In short, it's a bibliophile's dream world with something to offer for all interests.

USINGER'S SAUSAGES

Downtown/Third Ward/Central

1030 N Old World Third St.
Milwaukee, WI 53203
414-276-9105 | www.usinger.com

Go to Milwaukee's best-known "wurstmacher" and get a pound of tongue blood sausage to impress and/or appall your kids. Or get something else—they have wursts you've never heard of.

WISCONSIN CHEESE MART

Downtown/Third Ward/Central

215 W Highland Ave.
Milwaukee, WI 53203
414-272-3544 | www.wisconsincheesemart.com

Pick up a few crocks of cheese, or even a 10 oz. cheddar in the shape of a cow. This place even has a Cheese Bar to sample the goods. You're in Wisconsin. Cheese-eating is what WonderDads and their kids do.

ART SMART'S DART MART AND JUGGLING EMPORIUM

East Side/Riverwest/Brewers Hill

1695 N Humboldt Ave.
Milwaukee, WI 53202
414-273-DART | www.jugglingsupplies.net

Kites, boomerangs, darts, yo-yos, disc-golf discs, novelties, and, yes, even 60" fire staffs, can all be found at the Dart Mart and Juggling Emporium. It's the perfect stop on a lazy day or if you're trying to figure out something to do with the kids.

BOSWELL BOOK COMPANY

East Side/Riverwest/Brewers Hill

2559 N Downer Ave.
Milwaukee, WI 53211
414-332-1181 | www.boswellbooks.com

This independent book store, staffed by book lovers and former employees of the now-defunct Harry Schwartz Bookstore, is well-stocked and well-loved. Remember: WonderDads support local businesses! Downer Theater is next door for pre- or post-movie browsing!

BULLSEYE RECORDS

East Side/Riverwest/Brewers Hill

1627 E Irving Pl.
Milwaukee, WI 53202
414-223-3177

Whoa. Vinyl. They have CDs too but the main attraction is the records. Worth a stop if nothing more than to have your kids laugh at analog... and for you to bemoan the fact that no one cares much about album art anymore.

BURKE CANDY

East Side/Riverwest/Brewers Hill

3840 N Fratney St.
Milwaukee, WI 53212
414-964-7327 | www.burkecandy.com

Burke's doesn't have to compete with the candy aisle at the gas station, for it's in a class of its own. Give your kids a class on fine dining with the gourmet treats on offer.

COLLECTOR'S EDGE COMICS

East Side/Riverwest/Brewers Hill

2004 N Farwell Ave.
Milwaukee, WI 53202
414-272-5055 | www.collectorsedgecomics.com

Introducing your kids to comics is part of being a WonderDad. This is the place to do it.

CORY THE BIKE FIXER

East Side/Riverwest/Brewers Hill

2410 N Murray Ave.
Milwaukee, WI 53211
414-967-9446 | www.corythebikefixer.com

Milwaukeeans love Cory's for its good prices and friendly staff. The shop also offers customized bike maintenance classes – teach the kids how to take care of their bikes...or just let them rust out there in the lawn where they left them.

THE EXCLUSIVE COMPANY

East Side/Riverwest/Brewers Hill

1669 N Farwell Ave.
Milwaukee, WI 53202
414-271-8590

The idea of buying a CD or DVD is not as popular as a decade ago, but go old school and show your kids what they're missing. A nice selection of new and used CDs and DVDs at good prices—you even save more if you pay in cash. This place laughs in the face of internet downloads and credit cards. I hope they have the last laugh.

FISCHBERGER'S VARIETY

East Side/Riverwest/Brewers Hill

2445 N Holton St.
Milwaukee, WI 53212
414-263-1991

"Variety" is the operative word in this kinda-toy store that features retro, wooden, and tin toys among its eclectic mix of offerings. You don't go to Fischberger's with a list of things to get, but you will always walk out with a bag full of odds and ends that your kids (and you) somehow just can't live without

GLORIOSO BROS. CO. ITALIAN FOODS

East Side/Riverwest/Brewers Hill

1011 E Brady St.
Milwaukee, WI 53202
414-272-0540

This family-run grocery and deli is an East side institution. This new location offers seating by the expansive deli. Order a meatball sandwich (or a Human Torch if you're a tough guy) with a side of artichoke fritters and head down the aisles with the kids picking out some pizza dough and toppings for your homemade pizza night. The place has a gelato counter to boot!

RIVERWEST CO-OP GROCERY AND CAFÉ

East Side/Riverwest/Brewers Hill

733 E Clarke St.
Milwaukee, WI 53212
414-264-7933 | www.riverwestcoop.org

Housed in a former Schlitz tavern, this largely volunteer-run co-op sells local, organic, and vegan fare. An attached café in a converted garage serves up healthy organic and vegetarian/vegan soups and sandwiches. Think the kids will go for tofu ice cream? It's worth a shot.

STORES

STORES

UTRECHT ART SUPPLIES

East Side/Riverwest/Brewers Hill

2219 N Farwell Ave.
Milwaukee, WI 53202
414-220-9063 | www.utrechtart.com
Get some Sculpey clay and model a 1/18th-scale Devil's Tower. It sure beats using mashed potatoes and won't freak your kids out as much.

BOARD GAME BARRISTER

North Shore & North City

Bayshore Town Center
5738 N Bayshore Dr.
Glendale, WI 53217
414-963-2100 | www.boardgamebarrister.com
It's every WonderDad's responsibility to teach the kids how to play chess. Pick up a chessboard in this store that offers everything from chess and backgammon to card games to the nouveau favorites Apples to Apples and Settlers of Cataan.

COLLECTOR'S EDGE COMICS

North Shore & North City

7826 W Burleigh St.
Milwaukee, WI 53222
414-445-5055 | www.collectorsedgecomics.com
WonderDad is a superhero. Slay dragons, fly through the skies, and hang out with Jughead at this comic book store.

HAPPY HOBBY

North Shore & North City

7125 N 76th St.
Milwaukee, WI 53223
414-461-6013 | www.happyhobby.com
Erector sets, telescopes, yo-yos, rockets, RC cars, and plastic models can all be found here. It's the stuff of boyhood! Perfect for WonderDad-guided mischief.

LEARNING SHOP

North Shore & North City

Riverpoint Village
8665 N Port Washington Rd.
Fox Point, WI 53217
414-352-7010 | www.learningshop.com
With a focus on educational toys and four area locations, Learning Shop has a nice selection of toys and games that you won't find in the chain toy stores.

WHEEL AND SPROCKET
BIKE SHOP
North Shore & North City

6940 N Santa Monica Blvd.
Fox Point, WI 53217
414-247-8100 | www.wheelandsprocket.com

Don't know what a sprocket is? No problem at the largest bike stores in Wisconsin with three Milwaukee-area locations. A large selection of bikes (including tricycles), a knowledgeable and friendly staff, and an active role in the community all make Wheel and Sprocket worthy of a stop in, whether it be for a tune-up or to get your kid's first bike.

WINKIE'S
North Shore & North City

629 E Silver Spring Dr.
Whitefish Bay, WI 53217
414-964-2130

Inside you'll find a nice selection of unique gifts, housewares, stationary, seasonal items, and, of interest to the kids, a big candy counter and a great toy selection. Check out the Playmobil and Brio wooden toy offerings—they seem to have a complete set of everything and put the bigger box stores to shame.

AQUATICS
UNLIMITED
South Side/Fifth Ward/Walker's Point

3550 S 108th St.
Greenfield, WI 53228
414-543-2552 | www.bestfish.com

At some point, your kids are going to want a pet. Not yet ready to get a Cocker Doodle? Why not try some fish—or at least have a fun time looking at all that Aquatics Unlimited has on display. Be sure to check out the big hammerhead mounted on the wall above the cash register.

COLLECTOR'S
EDGE COMICS
South Side/Fifth Ward/Walker's Point

2330 S Kinnickinnick Ave.
Milwaukee, WI 53207
414-481-5055 | www.collectorsedgecomics.com

For whatever reason, new comics come out on Wednesdays. With video games releasing on Tuesdays and movies on Fridays, that leaves your Thursdays and Mondays free...

73

THE EXCLUSIVE COMPANY
South Side/Fifth Ward/Walker's Point

5026 S 74th St.
Greenfield, WI 53220
414-281-6644

The idea of buying a CD or DVD is going the way of the dodo, but go old school and show your kids what they're missing. This location is full of that retro record store feel, and a hip, helpful staff. If you're looking for that offbeat item you just know your kids will want to hold in their hands, not just their harddrive, this is the place.

GROPPI'S FOOD MARKET
South Side/Fifth Ward/Walker's Point

1441 E Russell Ave.
Milwaukee, WI 53207
414-747-9012 | www.ggroppifoodmarket.com

A true neighborhood market, this corner store has been in business since 1910. The deli is particularly good, and this WonderDad recommends the rueben panini. Be sure to have them toast it for you and then sit out on the outdoor patio and people-watch as you dig in.

LEARNING SHOP
South Side/Fifth Ward/Walker's Point

Southridge Plaza
5431 S 76th St.
Greendale, WI 53129
414-423-7294 | www.learningshop.com

With a focus on educational toys and four area locations, Learning Shop has a nice selection of toys and games that you won't find in the chain toy stores.

LOST WORLD OF WONDERS
South Side/Fifth Ward/Walker's Point

6913 W Oklahoma Ave.
Milwaukee WI 53219
414-328-4651 | www.lostwonders.com

Bring a treat for the cat Boo and peruse the stacks in this comic store. The website includes recommended reading lists for various age groups as well as for girls as an introduction to the world of comics and manga.

SOUTH SIDE TRAINS
South Side/Fifth Ward/Walker's Point

2633 W Kinnickinnick Ave.
Milwaukee, WI 53207
414-482-1566 | www.southsidetrains.com

Everybody loves a train. Tom, the owner, runs this one-man operation in Bay View where the train connoiseur can introduce his kids to the vast knowledge of Tom's years of collecting, building and operating model trains. Call for hours, as it's up to Tom when he's open.

WHEEL AND SPROCKET BIKE SHOP
South Side/Fifth Ward/Walker's Point

5722 S 108th St.
Hales Corner, WI 53130
414-529-6600 | www.wheelandsprocket.com

Don't know what a sprocket is? No problem at the largest bike stores in Wisconsin with three Milwaukee-area locations. A large selection of bikes (including tricycles), a knowledgeable and friendly staff, and an active role in the community all make Wheel and Sprockets worthy of a stop in, whether it be for a tune-up or to get your kid's first bike.

A HAIR FOR KIDS SALON
West Side & Wauwatosa

14023 W Greenfield Ave.
New Berlin, WI 53151
262-938-5999 | hairforkidssalon.webs.com

Get your kid's first haircut here in a variety of fun chairs, or, if you're feeling bold, hold a birthday party spa event for your daughter and her friends—complete with karaoke machines, dance floor, and dress up gowns.

AMERICAN SCIENCE AND SURPLUS
West Side & Wauwatosa

6901 W Oklahoma Ave.
Milwaukee, WI 53219
414-541-7777 | www.sciplus.com/storeDetail.cfm?store=3

Possibly one of the coolest/weirdest stores you'll ever enter. Need a bag of teddy bear eyes? A box o' bones? A sextant? You'll find them all at American Science and Surplus.

75

STORES

ART 'N ODDITIES
West Side & Wauwatosa

5833 W Lincoln Ave.
Milwaukee, WI 53219
414-329-2788 | www.artnoddities.com
Arts 'N Oddities is a colorful, fun gallery filled with an eclectic mix of items—lamps, paintings, furniture, jewelry, glassware, stuffed animals—that usually spark up a kid's interest and offer ideas to add a little sumthin-sumthin to your kid's room.

ARTIST AND DISPLAY
West Side & Wauwatosa

9015 Burleigh St.
Milwaukee, WI 53222
414-442-9100 | www.artistanddisplay.com
An established arts supply stop with a great selection of kid-specific items, no WonderDad should fail to unleash his kids' artist within.

COLLECTOR'S EDGE COMICS
West Side & Wauwatosa

6830 W Lincoln Ave.
West Allis, WI 53219
414-541-5055 | www.collectorsedgecomics.com
Marvel or DC? Let your kids decide at this venerable Milwaukee comic shop.

GIFT OF WINGS
West Side & Wauwatosa

9955 W St. Martins Rd.
Franklin, WI 53132
414-425-8002 | www.giftofwings.com
The parent store to the Veterans Park kite shop, this place is a celebration of aviation, offering everything from a tie with an F-14 Tomcat on it to a 23-foot indoor remote control blimp rental. Gift of Wings also hosts various kite-flying events throughout the year.

GOO GOO GAA GAA
West Side & Wauwatosa

Sendik's Towne Centre
18905 W Capitol Dr. Suite 100
Brookfield, WI 53045
262-790-6890 | www.googoogaagaa.com
For the younger kids—actually, for the ones that are so young that they'll probably have no memory of the place—Goo Goo Gaa Gaa offers up some unique furniture, artwork, rugs, and accessories to gussy up your baby's room.

GREENFIELD NEWS AND HOBBY

West Side & Wauwatosa

6815 Layton Ave.
Greenfield, WI 53220
414-281-1800 | www.greenfieldnewsandhobby.com

Rockets and models and trains, oh my! Take an art class. Join a model rocket club. Peruse the massive racks of magazines. It's all here.

HAPPY HOBBY

West Side & Wauwatosa

Two locations:
8021 W National Ave.
West Allis, WI 43214
414-453-3210
7821 W Burleigh St.
Milwaukee, WI 53214
414-444-0700 | www.happyhobby.com

With the stuff you need to complete just about any miniature construction project, these are the shops to visit when your kid comes to you with his Lego Taj Mahal and says, "what now, WonderDad?"

LEARNING SHOP

West Side & Wauwatosa

Two locations:
2911 Mayfair Rd.
Wauwatosa, WI 53222
414-475-9577
17435 W Blue Mound Rd.
Brookfield, WI 53045
262-789-6994
www.learningshop.com

With a focus on educational toys and four area locations, Learning Shop has a nice selection of toys and games that you won't find in the chain toy stores.

LITTLE READ BOOK

West Side & Wauwatosa

7603 W State St.
Wauwatosa, WI 53213
414-774-2665 | www.littlereadbook.com

A small, independent bookstore in a dying breed these days (RIP Harry Schwartz!). WonderDads supports it and its well-stocked selection of children's books located in downtown Tosa.

STORES

77

PUZZLE WORLD

West Side & Wauwatosa

12501 W Blue Mound Rd.
Brookfield, WI 53005
262-797-6302 | www.puzzleworld.com
Need a puzzle? PuzzleWorld's got it. From 24,000 piece monsters to a simple four-piecer and everything in between. It's great that stores like this exist.

WHEEL AND SPROCKET BIKE SHOP

West Side & Wauwatosa

13925 W Capitol Dr.
Brookfield, WI 53005
262-783-0700 | www.wheelandsprocket.com
Don't know what a sprocket is? No problem at the largest bike stores in Wisconsin with three Milwaukee-area locations. A large selection of bikes (including tricycles), a knowledgeable and friendly staff, and an active role in the community all make Wheel and Sprocket worthy of a stop, whether it be for a simple tune-up or to get your kid's first bike.

MARASCO'S CRAFT KING AND ROSE'S DOLL HOUSE

West Side & Wauwatosa

12750 W Capitol Dr.
Brookfield, WI 53005
Marasco's: 262-781-9660
Rose's: 262-373-0350
www.craftking.com
Forget about Barbie—this place is the real deal when it comes to doll houses. Need a miniature snub-nosed revolver for the crime scene you're working on in your daughter's doll house? Rose's has it...both with a wooden and a dark grip. Tough decision. And don't even get started trying to pick out a rug for your miniature parlor – there are hundreds to chose from. Dolls aside, the sheer amount of general arts and crafts supplies on hand is fantastic.

RAINBOW BOOKSELLERS
 West Side & Wauwatosa

5704 W Vliet St.
Milwaukee, WI 53208
414-774-7205 | www.rainbowbooksellers.com
The only children's-only bookstore in Milwaukee, Rainbow has irregular hours – make sure to call or check the website – but it's well worth a visit for unique books and a staff that knows children's books back and front.

SOMMERFELD'S TRAINS AND HOBBIES
West Side & Wauwatosa

12620 W Hampton Ave.
Butler, WI 53007
262-783-7797 | www.sommerfelds.com
I don't know the difference between a Z-scale and an H-scale train, but the friendly staff at Sommerfeld's—located just west of the train tracks – sure do. Closed Sundays and Mondays.

THE TOY DIMENSION
West Side & Wauwatosa

5925 W North Ave.
Milwaukee, WI 53208
414-476-5596
Need action figures? Toy Dimension has them. Lots and lots of them.

VILLAGE POPCORN
West Side & Wauwatosa

South end of the pedestrian bridge off State St. & Harwood Ave.
Wauwatosa, WI 53213
414-708-6707
This red wagon serves up popcorn, pretzels, ice cream, fresh-squeezed lemonade and is the perfect stopping point during a stroll through Tosa Village with the kids. Seasonal.

WHIMSIKIDZ
West Side & Wauwatosa

1346 N Wauwatosa Ave.
Wauwatosa, WI 53218
262-785-9012 | www.whimsikidz.com
The haircuts are on the pricier side here, but hey, you get what you pay for. For baby's first haircut, the folks at Whimsikidz are absolute pros. The kids really deserve better than your bowl-cut hack jobs, so spring for a Whimsikidz do before school photos this year. The photos on your desk and in your wallet all year will look that much better.

AMY'S CANDY KITCHEN
Ozaukee County & Points North

W62 N579 Washington Ave.
Cedarburg, WI 53012
262-376-0884 | www.amyscandykitchen.com
Amy specializes in gourmet candy apples—there are over 60 varieties dunked in chocolate, caramel, and rolled in most every kind of nut and candy (Gummy bears anyone?). The apples are huge and one is more than enough for sharing.

BERNIE'S FINE MEATS

Ozaukee County & Points North

119 N Franklin St.
Port Washington, WI 53074
262-284-4511 | www.berniesfinemeats.com
Load up on freshly made sausage at this butcher shop and show the kids that all meat doesn't come neatly wrapped in plastic.

DOWNTOWN DOUGH

Ozaukee County & Points North

W63 N658 Washington Ave.
Cedarburg, WI 53012
262-387-031 | www.downtowndough.com
Downtown dough has over 1600 cookie cutters—have your kids pick out a few (Hmmm...they came back with a velociraptor, fire hydrant, skull and bones, and karate guy cutter) then head home and have a fun afternoon baking cookies. You can even buy frozen dough if you're feeling particularly lazy.

EXPEDITION OUTDOOR SUPPLY

Ozaukee County & Points North

668 S Pier Dr.
Sheboygan, WI 53081
920-208-SURF (7873) | www.eosoutdoor.com
All your outdoors needs are available in this store located on the Sheboygan Harbor. Bike, kayak, and surfboard rentals are available, and you can even launch your kayak from the launch behind the store.

THE GAMEBOARD

Ozaukee County & Points North

1832 N 8th St.
Sheboygan, WI 53081
920-453-4263 | www.the-gameboard.com
What makes The Gameboard unique is that it offers board game rentals. Isn't it about time you taught the kids how to play Axis & Allies?

GLAZE POTTERY STUDIO

Ozaukee County & Points North

149 Green Bay Rd.
Thiensville, WI 53092
262-238-KILN (5456) | www.glazepottery.com
There are plenty of pottery-painting stores, but Glaze also offers glass fusing, jewelry making, and clay sculpting options for kids to make their own works of art (Beauty is in the eye of the WonderDad, in some cases). Classes are also offered and there's the Purple Frog lounge in front of the store that offers sodas and snacks.

PORTICO GIFT SHOP Ozaukee County & Points North

139 W Grand Ave.
Port Washington, WI 53074
262-284-6652
Out of eye patches? Stop in this store for all your pirate needs. The owners of this maritime-themed gift store started the annual Pirate Festival that takes place in the Port Washington lakefront the first weekend each June.

ALPACA ART POTTERY PAINTING Racine/Kenosha/Points South

5813 6th Ave.
Kenosha, WI 53140
262-657-4444 | www.alpacapottery.com
Stop in — no appointment necessary — and pick out a piece of pottery to paint. Wednesdays are ½-price studio fee for kids.

BENDTSEN'S BAKERY Racine/Kenosha/Points South

3200 Washington Ave.
Racine, WI 53405
262-633-0365 | www.bendtsensbakery.com
Racine is the kringle pastry capital of America. That alone is reason enough to visit. Founded in 1934, Bendtsen's is a third-generation family-run bakery that serves up an awesome handmade kringle using grandpa's original recipe from the old country. A small dining area is available for eating in, or order online through the website and they'll ship one out to you 2nd day air.

DOVER FLAG AND MAP Racine/Kenosha/Points South

323 Main St.
Racine, WI 53403
262-632-3133 | www.doverflag.com
While WonderDad may be the center of your kids' universe, they also should know that there's a bigger world out there. Buy them a map of Tierra del Fuego and a flag of Zimbabwe.

FIRED UP RACINE! Racine/Kenosha/Points South

320 Main St.
Racine, WI 53403
262-619-9234 | www.firedupracine.com
Unleash your inner artist with the kids in this paint-your-own-pottery studio located in downtown Racine. Pick from a variety of bowls, dishes, cups, and statues and have them create something that only a parent could love...and then bring it home, put it on your dresser, and store your change in it.

STORES

HEIM'S DOWNTOWN TOY STORE

Racine/Kenosha/Points South

5819 6th Ave.
Kenosha, WI 53140
262-652-8697 | www.downtowntoystore.com

Loaded with specialty toys, this local toy store is worth a visit. Scoops Ice Cream is right next door!

O&H DANISH BAKERY

Racine/Kenosha/Points South

Two locations:
1841 Douglas Ave.
Racine, WI 53402
262-637-8895
4006 Durand Ave.
Racine, WI 53405
262-554-1311 | www.ohdanishbakery.com

Odin was a WonderDad. Pay him tribute and eat like Viking warriors at one of the best bakeries in town. You haven't lived until you've had an O&H kringle. They're that good.

PAUL'S VIDEO ARCADE

Racine/Kenosha/Points South

Regency Mall
5564 Durand Ave.
Racine, WI 53406
262-554-1660 | www.paulsarcade.com

Alas, arcades have fallen on hard times. Paul perseveres, however, and it'd be a shame for the kids to never experience the joys of wandering an arcade with a pocketful of quarters. Getting them excited about Galaga and Ms. Pac-Man will be a tough sell, but much like Paul, WonderDads persevere.

SANDY'S POPPER ICE CREAM AND POPCORN

Racine/Kenosha/Points South

5503 6th Ave.
Kenosha, WI 53140
262-605-3202 | www.sandyspopper.com

Who doesn't like popcorn? Sandy's Popper offers a wide range of flavors (Salt and vinegar! Yeah!) and mixes along with large selection of ice cream.

SCOOPS! ICE CREAM AND CANDY
Racine/Kenosha/Points South

5819 6th Ave.
Kenosha, WI 53140
262-657-9866 | www.downtowntoystore.com
It's right next door to Heim's Downtown Toy Store. The question is: Do you get the ice cream before or after?

CUDDLES
Waukesha County & Points West

231 W Main St.
Waukesha, WI 53186
262-547-1060 | www.cuddles2u.com
Need a stuffed animal? Cuddles has it. It's attached to Martha Merrell's Bookstore—a quick escape route if you're suddenly feeling overwhelmed by giant teddy bears.

JEST FOR FUN JOKE SHOP
Waukesha County & Points West

265 W Main St.
Waukesha, WI 53186
262-544-5678 | www.jokeshop.us
The oldest and largest magic shop in Wisconsin, Jest for Fun offers magic tricks, gag gifts and practical jokes. Jeff, the store's owner, gives free demonstrations of his tricks and teaches regular magic lessons for kids every other Thursday night at the shop.

MARTHA MERRELL'S BOOKSTORE AND CAFÉ
Waukesha County & Points West

231 W Main St.
Waukesha, WI 53186
262-547-1060 | www.marthambooks.com
A nice independent bookstore—the last remaining of four locations founded by former head librarian of the Racine Public Library—Martha Merrell's has a nice selection of children's books and a knowledgeable, friendly staff. It's attached to Cuddles gift shop.

NEPTUNE COMICS
Waukesha County & Points West

2120 E Moreland Blvd.
Waukesha, WI 53186
262-544-2008 | www.neptunecomics.com
Who would win in a fight between Green Lantern and Superman? This is an important question that the kids should be prepared to answer. Start their education at Neptune Comics.

THE BEST DAD/CHILD
OUTDOOR PARKS
& RECREATION

BLUE MAX FISHING CHARTER
Downtown/Third Ward/Central

740 N Plankinton Ave.
Milwaukee, WI 53203
414-828-1094 | www.bluemaxcharters.com

Docked on the Riverwalk at the Rock Bottom Brewery, this charter service offers fishing and cruises on Lake Michigan. You and the kids will be telling fish stories about the one that got away in no time.

BIRDS OF PREY AT SCHLITZ AUDUBON NATURE CENTER
Downtown/Third Ward/Central

111 E Brown Deer Rd.
Milwaukee, WI 53217
414-352-2880 | www.schlitzaudoboncenter.com

Check out the falcons, hawks, owls, vultures, and eagles at the Sky Hunters Birds of Prey program offered weekly at the SANC. The person leading it is called a Raptor Handler. That's probably the best job title ever. Or just spend some time hiking along the 6+ miles of trails along Lake Michigan.

BRADFORD BEACH
Downtown/Third Ward/Central

2400 N Lincoln Memorial Dr.
Milwaukee, WI 53211
414-962-8809
www.bradfordbeachjam.com
www.milwaukeeairshow.com

Two snack shops, cabana and beach chair rentals, public restrooms, and volleyball courts complement this revitalized downtown beach on the shore of Lake Michigan. The water is cold and the bottom can be pebbly, but it's family-friendly and there's an active slate of activities throughout the season. Check out the website for details – the Family Day, Air and Water Show, and Polar Plunge are highlights – and don't forget to stop by Northpoint Burgers for some food and custard.

LAKEFRONT'S "GRAND NECKLACE OF PARKS"

Downtown/Third Ward/Central

Lake Park
3233 E Kenwood Blvd.
Milwaukee, WI 53211
414-962-8809 | www.countyparks.com

Frederick Law Olmsted, the guy who designed New York's Central Park, is largely responsible for Milwaukee County's wonderful park system, highlighted by Lake Park and the adjoining Back Bay and Veterans Parks to the south. The park is a great site for geocaching (www.geocaching.com) and letterboxing (www.letterboxing.org) as there are numerous hidden caches placed throughout the parks. Also, be sure to check out the prehistoric burial mound in the northwest corner of the park just east of the intersection of Locust St. and Lake Dr. It's unexcavated and is around 2,000 years old.

LAWN BOWLING AT LAKE PARK

Downtown/Third Ward/Central

3133 E Newberry Blvd.
Milwaukee, WI 53211
414-426-8085 | www.milwaukeelawnbowls.org

Seasonal. Located next to Lake Park Bistro in Lake Park, the Lawn Bowls Club offers open bowling most days throughout the summer. Stop by the clubhouse on Wednesdays at 6:30pm for a lesson in this august sport. Maybe they'll even explain the difference between lawn bowling and bocce.

MILWAUKEE BOAT LINE RIVER CRUISES

Downtown/Third Ward/Central

101 W Michigan St.
Milwaukee, WI 53203
414-294-9450 | www.mkeboat.com

WonderDads aren't all landlubbers. Plan a sightseeing, historical, or sunset cruise on Lake Michigan and along the Milwaukee, Menomonee, and Kinnickinnic Rivers aboard the mighty Voyageur and Iroquois. Well-prepared WonderDads will even bring a piece of line along and teach the kids how to tie a bowline and half-hitch.

NORTHPOINT LIGHTHOUSE
Downtown/Third Ward/Central

2650 N Wahl Ave.
Milwaukee, WI 53211
414-332-6754 | www.northpointlighthouse.org

Located in Lake Park, this lighthouse dates from 1855. Take a tour of the building and climb to the top of the 74-foot tower for a spectacular view of Lake Michigan and Milwaukee. Bring your binoculars, or better yet, your pirate telescope.

OUTDOOR ICE SKATING AT RED ARROW PARK
Downtown/Third Ward/Central

920 N Water St.
Milwaukee, WI 53202
414-289-8791 | county.milwaukee.gov/RedArrow11930.htm

Seasonal. Open from December through February, enjoy some outdoor skating in downtown Milwaukee at Red Arrow Park. The warming house has restrooms, lockers, and skate rentals, and the Starbucks next door is a perfect post-skate spot for a hot chocolate with the kids.

OUTDOOR MOVIES AT PERE MARQUETTE PARK
Downtown/Third Ward/Central

900 N Plankinton Ave.
Milwaukee, WI 53203
414-257-6100 | www.westown.org

Seasonal. Bring a blanket and snacks and enjoy a free family-friendly movie under the stars in the heart of downtown Milwaukee. Movies are shown on Fridays at dusk during the summer. Check the website for details and movie listings.

PADDLEBOAT ON VETERAN'S PARK LAGOON
Downtown/Third Ward/Central

801 N Lincoln Memorial Dr.
Milwaukee, WI 53202
414-217-7235 | www.juneauparkpaddleboats.com

After about five minutes, the novelty (and effort required) of paddling a boat will wear thin on the kids, but a WonderDad never shies away from a good workout. Stop by Alterra on the Lake afterwards for a snack and make an afternoon out of it.

PARADISE LANDING INDOOR
WATER PARK
Downtown/Third Ward/Central

Hilton Milwaukee City Center
509 W Wisconsin Ave.,
Milwaukee, WI 53202
877-543-7785 | www.paradiselanding.com

Located in the Hilton Milwaukee City Center, this tropical-themed water park is the perfect escape during Milwaukee's winter months. Paradise Landing is open to the public—though hotel guests get preference—so be sure to call ahead to determine accessibility and rates (which vary depending on the time of year).

BREW CITY
BIKE TOURS
East Side/Riverwest/Brewers Hill

Crank Daddy's Bike Works
2108 N Farwell Ave.
Milwaukee, WI 53202
414-336-9610 | www.brewcitybiketours.com

Bring your own bike and helmets (or rent them) and take a food or historical tour of Milwaukee. The tours usually last around two hours and offer discounted rates for kids 12 and under.

THE OAK LEAF TRAIL
East Side/Riverwest/Brewers Hill

Riverside Park
1500 E Park Place
Milwaukee, WI
county.milwaukee.gov/OakLeafTrail8289.htm

This 108-mile paved recreational trail winds its way around Milwaukee County and connects all of the major parks in the county in a "ribbon of green." Bike, walk, or skate along it from one of the East side access points in Riverside Park, or check the map on the website for a complete route map.

RENT A KAYAK AT THE URBAN
ECOLOGY CENTER
East Side/Riverwest/Brewers Hill

1500 E Park Place
Milwaukee, WI
414-964-8505 | www.urbanecologycenter.com

This park plays host to the Urban Ecology Center's "outdoor laboratory" and has a habitat-themed playground, climbing rock-wall, and a lagoon. Become a member of the Center and you can borrow equipment—canoes, bikes, camping equipment, snowshoes, gardening equipment and sleds among many others. Second Center is located in Washington Park.

89

ATWATER PARK
North Shore & North City

4000 N Lake Dr.
Milwaukee, WI 53211
414-847-2650 | villageofshorewood.org
It's small—only about three football fields in length—but this secluded sandy beach in Shorewood is a great place to get away from the crowds at Lake Park and Bradford Beach.

BROWN DEER "ORIGINAL" DISC GOLF COURSE
North Shore & North City

7625 N Range Line Rd.
Brown Deer, WI 53223
414-352-7502 | county.milwaukee.gov/DiscFrisbeeGolf9008.htm
This 18-hole disc golf course includes concrete tee pads and tournament-quality disc baskets. Free to play. Bring your own discs.

DOCTOR'S PARK
North Shore & North City

1870 E Fox Ln.
Milwaukee, WI 53217
414-352-7502
Along with Atwater Park, Doctor's Park is a hidden North Shore gem of a beach that's worth a visit if you're looking to get away from the crowds further south at Bradford Beach.

DRETZKA PARK "MEGA 27" DISC GOLF COURSE
North Shore & North City

12020 W Bradley Rd.
Milwaukee, WI 53224
414-354-8120 | county.milwaukee.gov/DiscFrisbeeGolf9008.htm
The county's best and biggest disc golf course, Dretzka Park offers a scenic and moderately wooded 27-hole course. Free to play. Bring your own discs.

GO FISHING...YEAR ROUND! North Shore & North City

McGovern Park
5400 N 51st St.
Milwaukee, WI 53218
Brown Deer Park
7835 N Greenbay Rd.
Milwaukee, WI 53209
DNR Urban Fisheries Hotline: 414-263-8494
county.milwaukee.goc/Fishing9141.htm
county.milwaukee.gov/IceFishing10254.htm

WonderDads love fish stories. Many Milwaukee County park lagoons offer fishing, and most are stocked by the Department of Natural Resources. When it gets cold, the real fun begins—a few even offer ice fishing. The DNR runs free spring and winter ice fishing clinics for children at various county parks. Check the website for details.

KLODE PARK   North Shore & North City

5900 Lake Shore Dr.
Whitefish Bay, WI 53217
www.klodepark.com

A well-appointed playground, restrooms, and large open field sit atop the bluff overlooking Lake Michigan in this overlooked and never-crowded park. A curving walkway and staircase both descend to the lake shore.

SCHULTZ AQUATIC CENTER   North Shore & North City

Lincoln Park
1301 W Hampton Ave.
Milwaukee, WI 53209
414-257-7230 | county.milwaukee.gov/Pools9145/LincolnAquatic.htm

This County-operated water park has something for kids of all ages, from a zero-depth pool to lap lanes to diving boards to water slides. It's also a great chance for WonderDads to show off their (former) washboard abs. A concession stand sells food and snacks—outside food and coolers are not permitted.

BOERNER BOTANICAL
GARDENS   South Side/Fifth Ward/Walker's Point

Whitnall Park
9400 Boerner Dr.
Hales Corner, WI 53130
414-525-5600 | www.boernerbotanicalgardens.org

Tucked away within Whitnal Park, the Botanical Gardens feature 40 acres of formal gardens including a rose, herb, and rock garden. The Garden's hour-long Growing Gardeners program is designed for preschoolers and their parents and includes stories, a snack, sing-alongs, and a hands-on gardening activity. The Gardens are closed November through April.

91

OUTDOOR PARKS

GASTRAU'S GOLF CENTER
South Side/Fifth Ward/Walker's Point

1300 E Rawson Ave.
Oak Creek, WI 53154
414-571-7002 | www.gastrausgolfcenter.com

A nice mini-golf course is playable at this golf center that has big overhanging heaters in its driving range so that the hardcore can drive golf balls years around. Making the par 2 by the waterfall is hardcore enough for WonderDads.

GO FISHING... YEAR ROUND!
South Side/Fifth Ward/Walker's Point

Scout Lake
5902 W Loomis Rd.
Greendale, WI 53129
Humboldt Park
3000 S Howell Ave.
Milwaukee, WI 53207
Wilson Park
1601 W Howard Ave.
Milwaukee, WI 53221
DNR Urban Fisheries Hotline: 414-263-8494
county.milwaukee.goc/Fishing9141.htm
county.milwaukee.gov/IceFishing10254.htm

WonderDads love fish stories. Many Milwaukee County park lagoons offer fishing, and most are stocked by the Department of Natural Resources. When it gets cold, the real fun begins as a few parks even offer ice fishing – be sure to check the signs to make sure the ice is safe to walk on. The DNR also runs free spring and winter ice fishing clinics for children at various county parks. Check the website for details.

GRANT PARK
South Side/Fifth Ward/Walker's Point

100 E Hawthorne Ave.
South Milwaukee, WI 53172
414-762-1550 | www.countyparks.org

Grant Park is huge. It has 4 playgrounds, beach access, soccer fields, tennis courts, a golf course, and trails that wind along Lake Michigan. The park in Wil-O-Way is a hidden gem if you're looking to not have to compete with a lot of other parents and kids. It's accessible via the entrance just south of Badger Ave., and has a big sandbox, swings, picnic tables, and a good-sized jungle gym with soft rubber floor. Be on the lookout for deer and rabbits, too.

GREEN FIELDS GOLF CENTER
South Side/Fifth Ward/Walker's Point

10600 W Layton Ave.
Greenfield, WI 53228
414-425-5152 | www.greenfieldsgolfcenter

Eighteen holes of well-maintained mini-golf are available at this full service golf center and driving range.

MILWAUKEE COUNTY SPORTS COMPLEX
South Side/Fifth Ward/Walker's Point

6000 W Ryan Rd.
Franklin, WI 53132
414-423-9267
www.county.milwaukee.gov/sportscomplex9051.htm
county.milwaukee.gov/DiscFrisbeeGolf9008.htm

Beat the winters in this 70,000-square-foot facility where you can rent volleyball, basketball, and indoor soccer courts by the hour. Softball and baseball batting cages are also available, and there's an adjacent outdoor nine-hole disc golf course.

RIVER FALLS FAMILY FUN CENTER
South Side/Fifth Ward/Walker's Point

5401 W Layton Ave.
Greenfield, WI 53220
414-281-2815

Go-carting, miniature golf, batting cages, and an indoor game room make for an easy fun time for WonderDads and their kids.

SOUTH SHORE PARK
South Side/Fifth Ward/Walker's Point

2900 S Shore Dr.
Milwaukee, WI 53207
414-257-PARK (7275) | www.countyparks.com

Head down on a Saturday morning during the summer for the best farmer's market in Milwaukee, or just take your kids to the great playground overlooking Lake Michigan. Better yet, head down to the rocky beach below the playground and teach your kids a fundamental WonderDad responsibility: skipping rocks.

OUTDOOR PARKS

WEHR NATURE CENTER

South Side/Fifth Ward/Walker's Point

9701 W College Ave.
Franklin, WI 53132

414-425-8550 | county.milwaukee.gov/WehrNatureCenter10115.htm

Located in Whitnall Park, the Nature Center includes 5 miles of trails that loop through varied landscapes including prairie, woodlands, wetlands, and savanna. Special family events throughout the year focus on the kid-approved gross, icky, and sticky: Frog Frolic, Bug Day, Reptile Day, Maple Sugar Days, Cider Day, and Owl Prowl.

COOL WATERS FAMILY AQUATIC PARK

West Side & Wauwatosa

Greenfield Park
2028 S 124th St.
West Allis, WI 53227
414-321-7530

county.milwaukee.gov/CoolWaters9156.htm

Open Memorial Day through Labor Day, this county-maintained water park has a zero-depth pool, tube and body waterslides, interactive water toys, sand volleyball courts, and a children's playground. Be warned – it gets very crowded. Also offers night swims after 6 pm with reduced admission.

CURRIE PARK GOLF DOME

West Side & Wauwatosa

3535 N Mayfair Rd.
Wauwatosa, WI 53222
414-453-1742 | www.curriegolfdome.com

Whack some balls throughout the winter in this heated indoor dome. When you, the kids (and the missus) are driving each other up a wall indoors on those frozen Wisconsin winter days, take the kids here for a dose of summer fun sure to relieve everyone's cabin fever.

DINEEN PARK DISC GOLF COURSE

West Side & Wauwatosa

6600 W Keefe Ave.
Milwaukee, WI 53216
414-871-4020 | county.milwaukee.gov/DiscFrisbeeGolf9008.htm

Bring your own discs and let 'em rip at this eighteen-hole disc golf course. It's free.

FISHING IN THE CITY
West Side & Wauwatosa

Greenfield Park
2028 S 124th St.
Milwaukee, WI 53227
McCarty Park
8214 W Cleveland Ave.
Milwaukee, WI 53219
Washington Park
1859 N 40th St.
Milwaukee, WI 53208
DNR Urban Fisheries Hotline: 414-263-8494
county.milwaukee.goc/Fishing9141.htm
county.milwaukee.gov/IceFishing10254.htm

These parks have stocked fish ponds, perfect places to introduce your young ones to your favorite outdoor pursuit.

FUN WORLD
West Side & Wauwatosa

620 Elizabeth Ct.
Brookfield, WI 53045
262-789-5370 | www.funworldbrookfield.com

It gets cold in Wisconsin. What do you do when you crave a nice summer's day outing but are under a foot of snow? Fun World has the answer...why else would you have an indoor Ferris wheel and mini-golf course?

HANK AARON STATE TRAIL
West Side & Wauwatosa

Western Trailhead: Pedestrian Bridge accessible from
Expos parking lot in Miller Park.
1 Brewers Way
Milwaukee, WI 53214
Eastern Trailhead: Lakeshore State Park Island adjacent
to the festival grounds
500 N Harbor Dr.
Milwaukee, WI 53202
414-274-4281 | dnr.wi.gov/org/land/parks/specific/hank_aaron

Starting at Lakeshore State Park near the festival grounds and connecting with the Oak Leaf Trail in Doyne Park by Miller Park, the Hank Aaron State Trail is one of the newest additions to the park system and provides a connection between Milwaukee's west side and the lakefront for walkers, runners, bikers, and skaters. Some on-street use is necessary but work continues to increase accessibility, safety, and convenience for users.

95

JACOBUS PARK
West Side & Wauwatosa

Main Entrance:
6501 W Hillside Ln.
Wauwatosa, WI 53213
Playground:
Honey Creek Parkway east off of N 68th St.
Wauwatosa, WI 53213
414-257-6100 | www.countyparks.com

A nice playground with rubberized floor and equipment for both toddlers and bigger kids, the park also includes a wading pool, sandbox, playing fields, picnic areas, and restrooms. Jacobus Park proper is a good-sized park, with hiking trails accessible past the playground and a nice pond for rock skipping (or grab chestnuts from up past the pond pavilion) and duck watching.

MILWAUKEE COUNTY ZOO
West Side & Wauwatosa

10001 W Blue Mound Rd.
Milwaukee, WI 53226
414-256-5412 | www.milwaukeezoo.org

The Milwaukee Zoo is home to the largest group of bonobos outside of the Congo. Awesome. This small but well-maintained zoo offers just enough to keep the kids interested without overstaying its welcome. It offers several Family Free days throughout the year—check the website for details.

MONARCH TRAIL
West Side & Wauwatosa

9480 W Watertown Plank Rd.
Wauwatosa, WI 53226
www.themonarchtrail.org

A stopping point for the annual Monarch butterfly migration, the Trail's butterflies usually arrive each year at the end of September, though times are variable depending on winds and weather – be sure to check out the website for more specific information. The trailhead starts in the Milwaukee County Parks Department parking lot across from the Mental Health center.

PUMP IT UP INFLATABLE PARTY ZONE
West Side & Wauwatosa

195 N Janacek Rd.
Brookfield, WI 53045
262-780-1010 | www.pumpitupparty.com

A "bouncy house" full of inflatable mazes and slides and obstacle courses, this national franchise is more focused on birthday party events than on open drop-in sessions, so be sure to check times for availability if you're not going to somebody's party. And you will. Sooner or later. This place hosts a lot of parties.

OUTDOOR PARKS

SWIM AT THE BEST WESTERN MIDWAY HOTEL

West Side & Wauwatosa

1005 S Moorland Rd.
Brookfield, WI 53005
877-664-3929 | www.midwayhotels.com/brookfield

A 10,000-foot tropical atrium and 80-degree pool make this a great weekend getaway with the kids, especially during the cold winter months. You can almost forget that it's -10 degrees outside.

SWISS TURNERS GYMNASTIC ACADEMY OPEN GYM

West Side & Wauwatosa

2214 S 116th St.
West Allis, WI 53227
414-321-4340 | www.swissturners.com

Open gyms on Saturdays from 6-8pm and preschool open gyms on Mondays, Wednesdays, and Thursdays. You can also rent the gym for birthday parties.

BAY BEACH AMUSEMENT PARK

Ozaukee County & Points North

1313 Bay Beach Rd.
Green Bay, WI
920-448-3365 | www.baybeach.org

The Green Bay Packers aren't the only thing that's owned by the city of Green Bay – the old-style charm of this amusement park by the bay (with no entrance fee, free parking, and 25 cent ride tickets!) has a history dating back to the 1890s and is currently going through several upgrades to include a new roller coaster. There's plenty of space and tables in the park so pack a cooler (that's even allowed!) and have a picnic! They also show free movies during the summer.

BLUE HARBOR RESORT

Ozaukee County & Points North

725 Blue Harbor Dr.
Sheboygan, WI 53081
920-457-9882 | www.blueharborresort.com

Offering both indoor and outdoor pools, the Blue Harbor Resort can be enjoyed year-round and includes seven waterslides and offers areas and activities appropriate for all ages, from its zero-depth pool complete with baby shipwreck to the 1,000-gallon "dipping ship" that pours a waterfall of water down on a four-story interactive lighthouse water fort. Public access is available for non-guests. Call for specific availability.

97

OUTDOOR PARKS

HARRINGTON BEACH STATE PARK

Ozaukee County & Points North

531 County Rd.
Belgium, WI 53004
262-285-3015 | www.dnr.state.wi.us

With a mile of sandy beach along the shores of Lake Michigan and a quarry lake, this 626-acre park also has camp grounds and participates in the Wisconsin Explorers, a tiered outdoors program geared for kids aged 3-5, 6-8, and 9 and up. Ask for the free activity booklet at the welcome center. Completing the activities earns the kids a patch!

HORSEBACK RIDING LESSONS

Ozaukee County & POints North

Lakefield Farm
1440 Lakefield Rd.
Grafton, WI 53024
262-375-4451 | www.lakefieldfarm.com

Whether they want to be a princess or a cowboy, WonderDads support their kids. Give them a head start in realizing their dreams by taking a father-child class on the real deal.

1860 LIGHT STATION AND LIGHTHOUSE MUSEUM

Ozaukee County & Points North

St. Mary's Hill
311 Johnson St.
Port Washington, WI
262-284-7240 | www.portwashingtonhistoricsociety.org

Think you and the kids can find Luxembourg on a map? This 1860 light station was restored in 2000 through funds provided by the government of Luxembourg as a memorial to US service men who fought for the Ducky's freedom in the Second World War. It depicts the life of a 19th-century light keep family. Open Saturdays and Sundays from May through October.

OZAUKEE COUNTY PIONEER VILLAGE

Ozaukee County & Points North

4880 County Highway 1
Saukville, WI 53080
262-377-4510 | www.co.ozaukee.wi.us/ochs/PioneerVillage.htm

Featuring a collection of over twenty buildings dating from the 1840s to the 1900s, Pioneer Village also has special events throughout the year including fiddling contests and Revolutionary War encampments (Take that, Civil War re-enactors!). Open Saturdays and Sundays. Children 5 and under are free and a family rate is available to save a few bucks.

OZAUKEE INTERURBAN TRAIL
Ozaukee County & Points North

W63 N643 Washington Ave.
Cedarburg, WI 53012
www.interurbantrail.us

A 30+ mile paved trail that runs along an old train line, the Interurban passes through most of the towns in the county which makes for great stopping points for lunch or snacks (The Chocolate Factory in downtown Cedarburg!). Restrooms and water fountains are also posted at regular intervals.

SNOWTUBING AT SUNBURST SKI AREA
Ozaukee County & Points North

8355 Prospect Dr.
Kewaskum, WI 53040
262-626-8404 | www.skisunburst.com

With a dedicated tubing area made up of 20 lanes, there's plenty of room to whizz down the slopes at this fun little resort just 15 minutes north of Milwaukee. Wunderbar for WunderDads!

SWING TIME FUN
Ozaukee County & Points North

W197 N10340 Appleton Ave.
Germantown, WI 53022
262-251-3311 | www.swingtimefun.com

Driving range, miniature golf, baseball and softball batting cages, and go-carts on the weekends (with some two-seater cars) are a staple of a WonderDads adventure.

TENDICK NATURE PRESERVE AND DISC GOLF COURSE
Ozaukee County & Points North

3919 Highway O
Saukville, WI 53080
262-284-8257
www.co.ozaukee.wi.us/planningparks/Tendick_Facilities.asp

The only eighteen-hole disc golf course in Ozaukee County. Free to play. Bring own discs.

ACTION TERRITORY
Racine/Kenosha/Points South

12345 75th St.
Kenosha, WI 53142
262-857-7000 | www.actionterritory.com

Go-carts, bumper boats, laser tag, batting cages, mini-golf, and bumper cars are all available at this one-stop fun center.

99

ALPINE VALLEY RESORT Racine/Kenosha/Points South

W2501 County Rd. D
Elkhorn, WI 53121
262-642-7374 | www.alpinevalleyresort.com

Non-Midwesterners will likely scoff at Alpine Valley and regale you with stories of winters in Vail. Well, we simple folk still rather like it, and despite the crowds, it's a good place to take the kids as it has a magic carpet conveyor belt lift on the bunny slope that's as non-intimidating as a ski lift can get.

BONG RECREATION AREA Racine/Kenosha/Points South

26313 Burlington Rd.
Kansasville, WI 53139
262-878-5600 | dnr.wi.gov/org/land/parks/specific/bong

People tend to snicker when they hear the name. They shouldn't. Major Dick Bong shot down 40 Japanese aircraft in World War II, is a Medal of Honor recipient, and remains the United States' highest-scoring ace in history. The recreation area named after the Wisconsin native is pretty awesome as well – it has 41 miles of trails spread over 4,515 acres.

JELLYSTONE PARK Racine/Kenosha/Points South

8425 State Rd. 38
Caledonia, WI 53108
262-835-2565 | www.jellystone-caledonia.com

This isn't really "roughing it"—but Jellystone Park offers just about everything that WonderDads and their kids need. A fishing pond, water park, playground, outdoor mini-theater, and game room will keep everyone entertained. Cabins, RV hook-ups, and tent campsites are all available.

KIDS' CONNECTION PLAYGROUND AT THE CALEDONIA Racine/Kenosha/Points South

Mount Pleasant Memorial Park
9614 County Rd. K
Franksville, WI 53126
262-886-0532 | www.mtpleasantwi.gov/Parks

This 20,000-square-foot monster of a playground includes a separate area for toddlers and includes multiple levels of slides, swings, sand boxes, and tunnels.

SPLASH AROUND IN THE LAUREL CLARK MEMORIAL FOUNTAIN Racine/Kenosha/Points South

30 6th St.
Racine, WI 53403

Named in honor of the astronaut and Racine-native killed in the Columbia shuttle disaster, the fountain and splash pad are a popular downtown summer play spot.

MULLIGAN'S MINI GOLF Racine/Kenosha/Points South

6633 Douglas Ave.
Racine, WI 53402
262-681-6464 | www.mulligansminigolf.com

Moonlight Madness with glow in the dark balls is offered every Wednesday night during the summers and Mulligan's plays host to professional mini-golf tournaments. It's also the site of the Guinness World Record for Most Holes of Miniature Golf Played in 24 Hours. It's 3,035.

NORTH BEACH Racine/Kenosha/Points South

1501 Michigan Blvd.
Racine, WI 53402
262-636-9131 | www.cityofracine.org/parks.aspx

This clean and expansive sandy beach includes a huge pirate-themed playground for the kids and includes a concession stand and rest rooms.

PETRIFYING SPRINGS COUNTY PARK Racine/Kenosha/Points South

4909 7th St.
Kenosha, WI 53144
262-857-1869 | www.co.kenosha.wi.us/publicworks/parks

Known to the locals as "Pets," this 360-acre park is the biggest in Kenosha County, and offers a little bit of everything – childrens' playground, sledding hill in the winter, horseshoe pits and sand volleyball courts, and several miles of great hiking trails through natural hardwood forests. There's also a natural spring along the Indian Springs Trail.

QUARRY LAKE PARK Racine/Kenosha/Points South

3800 Northwestern Ave.
Racine, WI 53405
262-637-6179

A former limestone quarry, the park is a popular spot for swimming and fishing. There is a picnic areas with grills, a concession stand with rest rooms, and kids 6 and under enter free during the summer, though you don't save much—the regular admission fee is a paltry buck.

SIX FLAGS GREAT AMERICA AND
HURRICANE HARBOR   Racine/Kenosha/Points South

1 Great America Parkway
Gurnee, IL 60031
847-249-4636 | www.sixflags.com

A forty-five minute drive south of Milwaukee, the amusement and water park are the stuff where unforgettable family memories are made. Remember: WonderDads don't puke after their third spin around the Ragin' Cajun. Be sure to take advantage of the Thrill Swap by letting the ride operator know—one parent can stay with the child while the other rides, and then swap places.

THE BIG BACKYARD Waukesha County & Points West

2857 S 160th St.
New Berlin, WI 53151
262-797-9117 | www.thebigbackyardwi.com

The name really says it all. It's a huge playground set up inside a warehouse in an industrial park—perfect for kids to let off some energy during a rainy day or during the winter. There are also a number of smaller playsets and riding toys.

COUNTRY SPRINGS HOTEL
WATER PARK   Waukesha County & Points West

2810 Golf Rd.
Pewaukee, WI 53072
262-547-0201 | www.countryspringshotel.com

Escape the winter in this year-round indoor water park that offers three-person boat rides, a zero-depth play area, and a lazy river. Day passes are available online.

FOX RIVER PARK
DISC GOLF COURSES Waukesha County & Points West

304 Ave.
Salem, WI 53168
262-857-1869 | www.co.kenosha.wi.us/publicworks/parks/locations.html

This county park offers two disc golf courses, the more challenging 18-hole Red Fox course and the more family-friendly 9-hole Red Fox course. Free score cards and course maps are available at the course entrances. Bring your own discs.

HELMAN'S DRIVING RANGE AND MINI GOLF
Waukesha County & Points West

N56 W19901 Silver Spring Dr.
Menomonee Falls, WI 53051
262-252-4447

This 18-hole course is relatively cheap and also has batting cages. What's not to like?

HILLCREST PARK
Waukesha County & Points West

2119 Davidson Rd.
Waukesha, WI 53186
www.ci.waukesha.wi.us/web/guest/prhillcrest

The website makes it sound lame, and the name of the park is straight out of some urban planner's cookie-cutter. Don't be fooled though, because the "Nike Hill" used to shoot missiles! From 1956-1971, Hillcrest Park was a Nike missile command and control center that was part of the system intended to defend Milwaukee against enemy bomber attacks during the Cold War. All that remains of the base are blast buildings, troop quarters, and a radar tower, but it's worth checking out.

LIME KILN PARK
Waukesha County & Points West

Downtown area south of Main St. and east of Appleton Ave.
Menomonee Falls, WI 53051
www.menomoneefalls.org/index.aspx?nid=149

Two 19th-century lime kilns along the Menomonee River highlight this park and site of the "original" waterfalls from which the village of Menomonee Falls was named. Victoria Falls doesn't have much to worry about.

PRAIRIEVILLE PARK ADVENTURE GOLF AND BATTING CAGES
Waukesha County & Points West

2507 Plaza Ct.
Waukesha, WI 53186
262-784-4653 | www.prairievillepark.com

Mini-golf, batting cages, and bumper cars. This is all-ages fun that any WonderDad can get behind. Prairieville also hosts events for the U.S. Pro Mini-Golf Association. Yes, there is such a thing.

SKATELAND
Waukesha County & Points West

1931 E Main St.
Waukesha, WI 53186
262-542-7971 | www.skate-land.com/waukesha.html

Family owned since 1955, Skateland offers Family admission specials on Thursday, all-you-can-eat pizza and soda night on Fridays, and free inflatable access for kids 10 and under on Saturdays and Sundays.

THE BEST DAD/CHILD
UNIQUE ADVENTURES

UNIQUE ADVENTURES

DOWNTOWN CARRIAGE RIDE
Downtown/Third Ward/Central

Various downtown locations
414-272-6873 | www.milwaukeecarriage.com

Up to six can enjoy a half-hour or hour-long carriage ride through downtown Milwaukee—or rent a twelve-seat wagon for a larger group. Reservations are made through the phone and there are several pick-up and drop-off locations.

FIND GERTIE THE DUCK AND HER SIX DUCKLINGS
Downtown/Third Ward/Central

E Wisconsin Ave. Bridge between N Water St. & N Plankinton Ave.
Milwaukee, WI

During the closing days of World War II, a duck nested beneath the Wisconsin Ave. bridge and created a national sensation as daily news reports gave updates. Gertie, as she came to be known, and two of her ducklings, Dee Dee and Pee Wee, have been immortalized in a four-foot tall bronze sculpture. Rosie and Millie are about fifty feet away on the East Riverwalk while Black Bill and Freddie are about the same distance in the other direction on the West Riverwalk.

JUMP THE SHARK WITH THE BRONZ FONZ
Downtown/Third Ward/Central

100 E Wells St.
Milwaukee, WI 53202

Your kids will have no idea who The Fonz is or that Happy Days took place in Milwaukee, but making a trip here is reason enough to teach them a bit of pop culture history. The statue itself is kind of creepy but unmistakable – you can find it on the eastern side of the Milwaukee River along the riverwalk off the west side of the Wells St. Bridge.

KETTLE KORN COWBOY
Downtown/Third Ward/Central

Various Locations
www.dougscowboykettlekorn.com

There's not much a whole lot better than freshly made kettle corn. Watching Cowboy Doug prepare it makes it taste even better—half of the kernels fly out of the kettle while he's feverishly making it, and he announces each new batch with a cowboy yell while banging on an iron triangle. Yee-ha! Check out his website for his schedule—he's a regular at several area farmers' markets—and you can also find his kettle corn at any of the local Sendik's Grocery Stores.

MILWAUKEE GHOST TOUR

Downtown/Third Ward/Central

Third Ward
Milwaukee, WI
414-807-7862 | www.milwaukeeghosts.com

WonderDads ain't afraid of no ghost. Take a walking tour through the historic Third Ward, or should I say, the "Bloody Third," with the knowledgeable "investigators" of Milwaukee Ghost Tours. They're serious about their trade and will even research your home or make referrals should you need a "clearing of your property." Zoinks!

MILWAUKEE TROLLEY

Downtown/Third Ward/Central

Various downtown locations
414-562-RIDE | www.milwaukeedowntown.com

Operating Wednesday through Saturdays during the summer, the free trolley is a fun way to get around downtown Milwaukee. With stops near most downtown attractions including the public museum, the festival park, the public market, and the riverwalk, there's no need to mess around with the car.

PIRATE CRUISE ON THE EDELWEISS

Downtown/Third Ward/Central

205 W Highland Ave.
Milwaukee, WI 53203
414-276-7447 | www.edelweissboats.com

The Edelweiss offers pirate-themed cruises complete with water balloon and squirt gun attacks. For the less adventurous, there are also historic sightseeing tours.

SEE THE ORIGINAL LORD OF THE RINGS MANUSCRIPTS!

Downtown/Third Ward/Central

Raynor Memorial Library Archives at Marquette University
1355 W Wisconsin Ave.
Milwaukee, WI 53201
414-288-7556 | www.marquette.edu/library/archives/tolkien.shtml

Purchased directly from J.R.R. Tolkien in 1957 for just £1500, Marquette University holds the largest collection of original Tolkien manuscripts in the world (over 11,000, including multiple working drafts of The Lord of the Rings and The Hobbit). "It's dangerous business...going out your front door. You step onto the road, and if you don't keep your feet, there's no knowing where you might be swept off to." WonderDads agree.

TAKE THE POLAR BEAR PLUNGE IN LAKE MICHIGAN ON NEW YEAR'S DAY
Downtown/Third Ward/Central

Bradford Beach
2400 N Lincoln Memorial Dr.
Milwaukee, WI 53211
847-778-0653 | www.polarplungemilwaukee.com

If your kids aren't impressed seeing their Speedo-clad WonderDad jump into Lake Michigan at noon on New Year's Day, I'm not sure what would. Join the thousands of folks – participants and spectators alike – who take part in this surprisingly well-organized annual event. Beware the guy in the Borat suit...

TEDDY ROOSEVELT WAS SHOT IN MILWAUKEE!
Downtown/Third Ward/Central

Hyatt Hotel Lobby
333 W Kilbourn Ave.
Milwaukee, WI 53203
414-276-1234

The bundle of papers containing the speech Roosevelt was going to give that night slowed down the round, though the bullet still lodged into his chest – and remained there until the day he died. Roosevelt, ever the Rough Rider, still gave his speech that night. A plaque in the lobby of the Hyatt Hotel marks the spot of the attempted assassination at the hand of the dastardly John Schrank, a New York saloon keeper.

TOUCH THE STONE IN THE ST. JOAN OF ARC CHAPEL
Downtown/Third Ward/Central

Marquette University
1355 W Milwaukee Ave.
Milwaukee, WI 53233
414-288-6873 | www.marquette.edu/chapel

Disassembled piece by piece and rebuilt on the Marquette campus in 1965, this 15th century French chapel contains a stone that Joan of Arc stood upon while praying. Ever since, legend has it that it has been colder than the stones surrounding it. Touch it and find out!

VISIT THE BIRTHPLACE OF THE AMERICAN LEAGUE
Downtown/Third Ward/Central

Intersection of North Old World 3rd St. and West Kilbourn Ave.

Marker located on the 4th fence post from the corner of the parking lot Milwaukee, WI.

Check out the plaque in the parking lot of the Milwaukee Journal Sentinel Building. It used to be a hotel, and on the site in 1900 the American League was formed. Milwaukee fortunately can't claim the designated hitter rule along with this distinction—that black day came much later.

WATCH AN OLDIE AT THE CHARLES ALLIS ART MUSEUM
Downtown/Third Ward/Central

1801 North Prospect Ave.
Milwaukee, WI 53202
414-278-8295 | www.cavtmuseums.org

Think your kid can handle a black and white movie shown from a 16mm projector in an old Milwaukee Tudor-style mansion? Could they rally for a December showing of Miracle on 34th St.? Maybe? Check out the schedule on the website and make the call. Movies are shown every other Wednesday at 7:30 pm. The museum also offers a Children's Workshop arts and crafts series.

CREAM CITY RICKSHAWS
East Side/Riverwest/Brewers Hill

Various East Side and Downtown locations
414-272-RIDE | www.creamcityrickshaw.com

Cream City Rickshaws play a dangerous game. They don't charge rates but instead rely upon tips to keep them pedaling. I suppose it works out all right – they've been around for few years now – but we like having them in Milwaukee so don't stiff your pedicab "driver" after he's just lugged you and the kids around town. Flag them down if you see them around town or call to arrange a ride.

CRUISE BY THE BOAT HOUSE
East Side/Riverwest/Brewers Hill

3138 N Cambridge Ave.
Milwaukee, WI 53211

Officially named the Edmund B. Gustorf House, this 1922 home is in the shape of...a boat. There's even a little light house next to it. There's not much to do except drive by it – it's still maintained as a private residence —but it's certainly a weird little oddity that will get a laugh out of the kids.

MILWAUKEE'S SUPERHERO

East Side/Riverwest/Brewers Hill

Riverwest, WI
www.the-watchman.webs.com

The Watchman, Milwaukee's very own superhero and member of the Great Lakes Heroes Guild, conducts safety patrols on the streets of Riverwest armed with a flashlight, pepper-spray, and a cell phone ready to dial 911. He has also run a toy drive over the holidays for the past several years. Look for his red mask and combat boots on the streets of Riverwest after dark on the weekends.

HURLING AT BROWN DEER PARK

North Shore & North City

Brown Deer Park
4920 W Green Brook Dr.
Brown Deer, WI 53224
414-297-9490 | www.hurling.net

The Irish sport of hurling is of prehistoric origin (cavemen played it!) and to the average American looks like an unholy mix of baseball, football, soccer, and golf. Milwaukee is home to the largest hurling club in North America. Who knew? Matches are also held at Kletzsch Park in Glendale.

MILWAUKEE POLICE HISTORICAL SOCIETY

North Shore & North City

6680 N Teutonia Ave.
Milwaukee, WI 53209
414-935-7190

Based at the Fire and Police Academy, this "museum" consists of two long rows of display cases on the first floor of the Academy. The public is welcome to take a look during normal business hours.

WHITEFISH BAY COMMUNITY CHESS CLUB

North Shore & North City

Roundy Baptist Church
1250 E Hampton Rd.
Whitefish Bay, WI 53217
262-573-5624 | www.wisconsinscholasticchess.org

Affiliated with the Wisconsin Scholastic Chess Federation, the Whitefish Bay Club offers weekly chess and instruction for kids as young as kindergarten, and additionally looks for volunteers to assist with supervision and coordination of the events.

ALLEN-BRADLEY CLOCK TOWER
South Side/Fifthe Ward/Walker's Point

1201 S 2nd St.
Milwaukee, WI 53204
414-382-2000

Milwaukee has the largest 4-sided clock face in the world, measuring twice the size of Big Ben. Take that, London! The minute hands are twenty feet long and weigh 590 pounds. The face also lights up at night and a smaller tower to the west displays the temperature. Pretty cool.

DOG SLEDDING IN WHITNALL PARK
South Side/Fifthe Ward/Walker's Point

Door County Sled Dogs
5879 S 92nd St.
Franklin, WI 53130
414-967-9677 | www.doorcountysleddogs.com

Answer the call of the wild and mush! The fee includes a visit with the dogs, picture taking, and a dog sled ride around the trail. Sled rides along the Milwaukee lakefront are also offered on occasion.

FATHER OF QWERTY GRAVESITE
South Side/Fifthe Ward/Walker's Point

Forest Home Cemetery
2405 W Forest Home Ave.
Milwaukee, WI
www.foresthomecemetery.com

Why is it that we know that Alexander Graham Bell invented the telephone and Thomas Edison the lightbulb, but we've forgotten about poor Christopher Latham Sholes, the inventor of the typewriter and the QWERTY keyboard? Pay homage to the forgotten hero by sending someone a text from his gravesite. There's also a historical society marker downtown at the corner of North 4th and West State St.s.

IRON WELL PUMP
South Side/Fifthe Ward/Walker's Point

1710 E Pryor St.
Milwaukee, WI 53204

Milwaukee gets its tap water from Lake Michigan. Everywhere, that is, except for the artesian water well in Bay View. Dug in 1882, the Iron Well water comes from an aquifer—not from Lake Michigan—and is the last remaining public well in the city. The hand pump is sadly gone—it has been replaced with an electric pump—and the water is regularly tested by the health department and DNR.

LAKE MICHIGAN LAKE EXPRESS FERRY
South Side/Fifth Ward/Walker's Point

2330 S Lincoln Memorial Dr.
Milwaukee, WI 53207
866-914-1010 | www.lake-express.com

This seasonal high-speed ferry offers daily service between Milwaukee and Muskegon, Michigan. The trip takes about two and a half hours. P.S. Don't miss the ferry on the way back—you cross from the Central to the Eastern time zone during the crossing.

CANDY CANE LN.
West Side & Wauwatosa

West Allis, WI
www.maccfund.com

Encompassing over 300 homes in the blocks in between 92nd and 96th Streets (and bound by Oklahoma Ave. on the south and Montana Ave. on the north), Candy Cane Ln. is a Griswoldian ode to holiday excess. The Christmas light extravaganza runs through most of December and it's completely free (though donations are accepted for the Midwest Athletes Against Childhood Cancer).

TRAINFEST
West Side & Wauwatosa

Wisconsin Exposition Center
8200 W Greenfield Ave.
West Allis, WI 53214
www.trainfest.com

The largest operating model railroad show in the country is held each November at the Wisconsin State Fair Grounds. With over 50 layouts and a big focus on activities for kids that include a circus train ride, Lego Build and Play area, and storytime, it's something not to be missed. Kids get in free with a coupon available at the website. The conductors cap and suspenders will cost extra.

WADHAM'S GAS STATION
West Side & Wauwatosa

Northwest corner of S 76th St. and National Ave.
West Allis, WI

Built in 1927, this gas station is in the shape of a pagoda. That's it. That's all it is. A gas station. In the shape of a pagoda.

WOOD NATIONAL CEMETERY

West Side & Wauwatosa

5000 W National Ave.
Milwaukee, WI 53295
414-382-5300
www.cem.va.gov/cerns/nchp/wood.asp

Located on the grounds of the Veterans Administration Medical Center, the cemetery has interments dating from the 1860s and includes five Civil War Medal of Honor recipients. The VA Center's Reclaiming Our Heritage organization additionally offers an annual nighttime lantern tour of the cemetery.

BIRTHPLACE OF FLAG DAY

Ozaukee County & Points North

County Rd. I (1/2 mile east of County Rd. H)
Waubeka, WI 53021

Flag Day was first formally celebrated in 1885 in this schoolhouse in the middle of nowhere. Check out the marker and restored schoolhouse, and perhaps organize the kids and begin a campaign to make it an official federal holiday. Nobody wants to work on Flag Day!

LAMBEAU FIELD TOUR

Ozaukee County & Points North

1265 Lombardi Ave.
Green Bay, WI 54304
Tours: 920-569-7513
Hall of Fame: 920-569-7512
Curly's Pub: 920-965-6970
Pro Shop: 920-569-7510
www.lambeaufield.com

Green Bay, Wisconsin has no business having a professional football team. It has a population of just over 200,000 people, for Pete's sake. Yet one trip to the city and you'll understand. Take the kids up to Lambeau while they're young and impressionable and ensure that they don't become Bears fans. Round out the day at Lambeau with lunch at Curly's Pub, then swing by the Pro Shop and the Packers Hall of Fame.

LAST COVERED BRIDGE IN WISCONSIN!

Ozaukee County & Points North

1700 Cedar Creek Rd.
Cedarburg, WI 53012
262-284-8257 | www.co.ozaukee.wi.us

It's built with no nails. Take that, Madison County! While you can no longer drive through it, its 120-foot span is open to foot traffic and the bridge now serves as a county park.

PORT WASHINGTON PIRATE FESTIVAL

Ozaukee County & Points North

Port Washington Lakefront
126 E Main St.
Port Washington, WI 53074
262-388-9762 | www.portpiratefestival.com

Pirates invade downtown Port Washington for this annual event held during the first full weekend in June. A parade, fireworks, treasure hunt, thieves marketplace, activities for kids, and a lot of folks dressed up like Jack Sparrow highlight this free lakefront event.

SPUTNIKFEST IN MANITOWOC

Ozaukee County & Points North

610 N 8th St.
Manitowoc, WI 54220
920-686-3090 | www.sputnikfest.com

A brass ring in the middle of the street marks the spot where the Soviet Sputnik IV satellite – or a 20cm by 8cm piece of it anyway – crashed back to earth after re-entry in 1962. The annual Sputnikfest, complete with Miss Space Debris pageant, is held every September to commemorate the event.

STUMPF'S U-CUT CHRISTMAS TREE FARM

Ozaukee County & Points North

340 Horns Corner Rd.
Cedarburg, WI 53012
262-375-6351 | www.ucuttrees.com

Head over to Stumpf's and cut down your own tree for the holidays. The kids will probably get cold and begin to question the fun of this fatherly endeavor – there's a heated barn with hot apple cider to help. Open Fridays, Saturdays, and Sundays from Thanksgiving to Christmas.

WISCONSIN AUTOMOTIVE MUSEUM

Ozaukee County & Points North

147 N Rural St.
Hartford, WI 53027
262-673-7999 | www.wisconsinautomuseum.com

Hartford was home to the Kissel Motor Car Company from 1906 until 1930, and several of the few remaining "Kissel Kars" are on display, as well as several Nash Motor cars from the former Kenosha-based company. A huge model train layout and a still-operational 250-ton steam locomotive from 1913 are also among the things to see.

WRITE A LETTER (PREFERABLY AN ODE) TO YOUR FAVORITE GREEN BAY PACKER
Ozaukee County & Points North

Attention: Individual Player/Coach Name

Green Bay Packers

P.O. Box 10628, Green Bay WI 54307-0628

Dear Clay Matthews: You run real speedy. Your locks flow like a Greek diety. The earth shakes with each sack. Please write back. Your fan, Little Johnny.

KENOSHA ELECTRIC STREETCARS
Racine/Kenosha/Points South

Joseph McCarthy Transit Center

725 54th St.

Kenosha, WI 53140

262-653-4290 | www.kenoshastreetcarsociety.org

Costing only 50 cents for adults and a quarter for kids, ride one of the five operational historic streetcars along a scenic two-mile route through downtown Kenosha.

MARS' CHEESE CASTLE
Racine/Kenosha/Points South

2800 120th Ave.

Kenosha, WI 53144

1-800-566-6147 | www.marscheese.com

The name really says it all. It's certainly kitschy, hokey, and touristy, but that's all part of the appeal. The assortment of cheeses is phenomenal and your kids will love sampling chocolate fudge cheddar and buffalo chicken cheese. There's a deli counter as well.

ROOT RIVER STEELHEAD TROUT FACILITY
Racine/Kenosha/Points South

Lincoln Park

2701 Domanik Dr.

Racine, WI 53404

262-884-2300 | dnr.wi.gov/fish/lakemich/rootriver.htm

Trout and salmon don't successfully naturally reproduce in Wisconsin waters, so this egg-gathering station supports the stocking of these fish in Lake Michigan. It has a fish ladder and observation window to view the fall and spring migrations, and while the facility does not offer regular tours, check the website for open house events or just wander the grounds on a self-guided tour.

UNIQUE ADVENTURES

UNIQUE ADVENTURES

CIRCUS WORLD
Waukesha County & Points West

500 Water St.
Baraboo, WI 53913
608-356-8341 | circusworld.wisconsinhistory.org

The Ringling Bros. Circus was founded in Baraboo in 1887, and Circus World continues the tradition! Seasonal circus performances as well as interactive kids' events make for a great trip. The Dells are close-by, so it's a no-brainer.

DR. EVERMOR AND THE FOREVERTRON
Waukesha County & Points West

S7703 US Hwy. 12
North Freedom, WI 53951
608-219-7830 | www.worldofevermor.com

This place is impossible to describe. Visit the world's largest scrap metal sculpture garden and witness one man's dream of a Victorian steampunk future. Located behind Delaney's Surplus and across the street from the old Badger Ammunition Plant.

INTERNATIONAL CLOWN HALL OF FAME
Waukesha County & Points West

102 4th Ave.
Baraboo, WI 53913
608-355-0321 | www.theclownmuseum.org

Yes, Bozo is in here. Recently moved from Milwaukee's State Fair Grounds, the Clown Hall of Fame is open Wednesday through Saturday.

LITTLE AMERRICKA AMUSEMENT PARK
Waukesha County & Points West

700 E Main St.
Marshall, WI 53559
608-655-3181 | www.littleamerricka.com

Run by the Merrick family (Get it?), this clean, well-run, and well-loved amusement park in the middle of nowhere is a great way to spend the day on "classic" rides with younger kids. Highlights are the small gauge train, mini-golf course, and the old wooden roller coaster. Prices (both entrance fees and food) are shockingly low and, even more refreshingly, you can even bring in your own coolers and eat lunch at one of the picnic tables around the park.

WILMOT MOUNTAIN
SKI RESORT

Waukesha County & Points West

11931 Fox River Rd.
Wilmot, WI 53192
262-862-2301 | www.wilmotmountain.com

This small ski resort is a great place for beginners and kids, though it can get crowded both waiting in lift lines and renting equipment. Wilmot offers a Winter Wonderlands ski-play area for children aged 4 to 9 and children 6 and under ski for free.

UNIQUE ADVENTURES

THE BEST DAD/CHILD
SPORTING EVENTS

BEACH VOLLEYBALL

Bradford Beach
2400 N Lincoln Memorial Dr.
Milwaukee, WI 53211
414-962-8809 | www.bradfordbeachjam.com
Bradford Beach hosts several professional events every season so be sure to head down and cheer on Iceman and Slider as they take on Goose and Maverick...or something like that. If volleyball's not your bag, there's also rugby, wiffleball, and sand soccer events. Wiffleball, huh? Weird.

BREWCITY BRUISERS ROLLER DERBY

US Cellular Arena
400 W Kilbourn Ave.
Milwaukee, WI 53203
414-908-6001
www.uscellulararena.com
www.brewcitybruisers.com
Matches are called bouts. Players play under pseudonyms like Femelde-hyde and Becky the Butcher. A percentage of the proceeds from events are given to charities and admission discounts are given for donating select items at the door. What's not to like? Go watch some roller derby!

MILWAUKEE BUCKS BASKETBALL

1001 N Fourth St.
Milwaukee, WI 53202
414-227-0700
bradleycenter.com
www.milwaukeebucks.com
Fear the deer! The Bucks won the NBA championships in 1971 behind the awesomeness of Lew Alcindor and Oscar Robertson. They haven't won since. Will this year be their return to glory? Join Bango and the fans at the Bradley Center and cheer on the Bucks! Afterwards, write a fan letter to Brandon Jennings about improving his outside shot. You can mail it to him here: Attn: Brandon Jennings, Milwaukee Bucks, Bradley Center, 1001 N. 4th St. Milwaukee, WI 53202-1314.

MILWAUKEE MUSTANGS ARENA FOOTBALL

Bradley Center
1001 N Fourth St.
Milwaukee, WI 53202
800-MKE-IRON | www.mkeiron.com
With the Packers and Badgers seasons long over, there's still football to be had during the spring and summer in Milwaukee. Attendance is unfortunately low and the Mustang's off-the-field financial issues seem to dominate the news more than its exploits on the field (and they're a pretty good team by AFL standards).

MILWAUKEE WAVE INDOOR SOCCER

US Cellular Arena
400 W Kilbourn Ave.
Milwaukee, WI 53203
414-908-6001
www.uscellulararena.com
www.milwaukeewave.com

Keith Tozer, head coach of the Milwaukee Wave, is a legend in soccer circles. The Milwaukee Wave professional indoor soccer team has won four league championships and Tozer has been named Coach of the Year eight times. Support professional soccer in Milwaukee and check out the Wave. It's fast, a lot of goals are scored, and you can get really close to the action. Join the Wave Kid's Club for a host of cool benefits including t-shirts, autographs, and human tunnel access before a game!

MARQUETTE GOLDEN EAGLES

Bradley Center
1001 N Fourth St.
Milwaukee, WI 53202
414-288-GOMU (4668)
www.gomarquette.com
bradleycenter.com

The Golden Eagles have a marquee men's basketball program that plays host to 18,000 screaming fans at the Bradley Center, but it also offer so much more to the young sports fan. With facilities around Milwaukee that include the on-campue Al McGuire Center, Marquette athletes compete in men's and women's basketball, soccer, track and field, tennis, women's volleyball, and men's golf.

UNIVERSITY OF WISCONSIN-MILWAUKEE PANTHERS

US Cellular Arena
400 W Kilbourn Ave.
Milwaukee, WI 53203
414-908-6001
www.uwmpanthers.cstv.com
www.uscellulararena.com

The UWM Panthers men's basketball team plays out of the US Cellular Arena. Check out their on-again annual matchup against cross-town Marquette or Horizon conference rivals like Butler and Loyola. Panther athletes additionally compete in men, and women's soccer, track and field, swimming and diving, men's baseball, and women's volleyball, tennis, and basketball.

SPORTING EVENTS

BREWERS GAME AT MILLER PARK

1 Brewers Way
Milwaukee, WI 53214
www.milwaukeebrewers.com

It doesn't get much better than a Dad, his kids, and a baseball game. Take them to Miller Park for a game and don't forget that you can bring food and drinks into the park (along with your gloves, of course) – always a good option to save some money. Even better yet, make a complete day of it and tailgate in the parking lot before the game.

SHEBOYGAN ATHLETICS SEMI-PRO BASEBALL

Wildwood Baseball Park
S Wildwood Ave.
Sheboygan, WI 53081
920-458-6377 | www.sheboyganbaseball.com

A member of the Wisconsin State League, the Athletics play close to 30 games a season – and have been doing it since 1963. Like you need an excuse to bring the kids to a baseball game.

GO WATCH A MINOR LEAGUE BASEBALL GAME!

Beloit Snappers
2301 Skyline Dr.
Beloit, WI 53511
608-362-2272 | www.snappersbaseball.com

Don't get me wrong, a game at Miller Park is great for a Milwaukee WonderDad, but the hot dogs somehow taste better and the air feels a little fresher at a minor league baseball game. Plus, tickets on the third base line won't cost a fortune, and the kids are 10 times more likely to get an autograph before the game.

WISCONSIN BADGERS FOOTBALL GAME AT CAMP RANDALL

1440 Monroe St.
Madison, WI 53711
www.uwbadgers.com

Camp Randall is a monster – it seats over 80,000 people. And it's old – the Badgers have used the field since 1895. So put on your red and take in a game at the venerable stadium with the kids. It's a Wisconsin requirement.

ABOUT THE AUTHOR

Josh Olson, an aspiring WonderDad, lives in Wauwatosa, Wisconsin.

DEDICATIONS

To my wife Meg who supported me in this endeavor despite two new jobs, a new house, and a new WonderKid. She's a WonderWife indeed.

To my daughters Amelia and Bridget for teaching me what it means to be a kid again. ¡Les saludo, muchachas!

To Milwaukee.